The Narcissism of Empire

Loss, Rage and Revenge
in Thomas De Quincey,
Robert Louis Stevenson,
Arthur Conan Doyle,
Rudyard Kipling
and Isak Dinesen

Diane Simmons

sussex
ACADEMIC
PRESS

BRIGHTON • *PORTLAND*

2 4 6 8 10 9 7 5 3 1

First published 2007 in Great Britain by
SUSSEX ACADEMIC PRESS
PO Box 139
Eastbourne BN24 9BP

and in the United States of America by
SUSSEX ACADEMIC PRESS
920 NE 58th Ave   Suite 300
Portland, Oregon 97213–3786

British Library Cataloguing in Publication Data
A CIP catalogue record for this book is available from the British Library.

Library of Congress Cataloging-in-Publication Data
Simmons, Diane, 1948–
   The narcissism of empire : loss, rage, and revenge in
      Thomas De Quincey, Robert Louis Stevenson,
      Arthur Conan Doyle, Rudyard Kipling, and Isak Dinesen
   / by Diane Simmons.
   p. cm.
   Includes bibliographical references and index.
   ISBN 1-84519-156-0 (alk. paper; h/c)
   ISBN 1-84519-157-9 (pbk.)
   1. English fiction—19th century—History and criticism.
   2. Imperialism in literature. 3. English fiction—20th
   century—History and criticism. 4. Popular literature—
   Great Britain—History and criticism. 5. Narcissism in
   literature. 6. Colonies in literature. I. Title.
PR868.I54S56 2006
823'.809358—dc22

                                                    2006014015

Typeset & designed by S A P, Brighton & Eastbourne
Printed by TJ International, Padstow, Cornwall
This book is printed on acid-free paper.

CONTENTS

ILLUSTRATIONS

PREFACE

"Love's loss was empire's gain"

Modern theories of personality hold that children who do not get enough of the right kind of emotional support develop an eternally hungry psyche, a psychic injury from which they seek to recover by dominating others in fantasy and reality. In societies where such injury is common, the attempt to buttress an insecure self-image by dominating other individuals, other groups, and even other nations can be widespread and viewed as quite normal. But while soldiers, administrators and politicians often know to bury or at least camouflage their fears and desires, inner fantasies are the necessary ingredients of literature. For that reason works of popular fiction have always offered the opportunity to probe the mind of an age.

Language is a "socially shared imaginative space," Marshall Alcorn has written, "where narcissistic needs are shaped and explored;" writing is a "powerful medium for transferring narcissistic needs into social space" (17). And psychologist Erik Erikson believes that the stories people love tell us a great deal about the fantasies of writer and reader alike: "A literary theme, to be convincing, need not be true; it must sound true, as if it reminded one of something deep and past" (*Childhood* 331).

The immense popularity of the works to be studied in this book suggests that the fantasies they contain struck a particular chord with a whole nation of readers, and that we may find in them a glimpse of some of the psychic needs that fuel the desires of imperial dominance.

Thomas De Quincey, Robert Louis Stevenson, Arthur Conan Doyle, Rudyard Kipling and Isak Dinesen were widely read during the age of British imperialism and all continue to be read today. Millions of people have viewed their works with approval and affection, and millions have used these stories to participate vicariously in the imperial project. Rudyard Kipling's stories and poems, for example, are frequently described as the medium through which empire saw itself, and Thomas De Quincey's mad screeds against the Chinese, whom he viewed as being both laughably weak and cunningly sinister, helped set the stage for stereotypes that have continued up to the present. Arthur Conan Doyle's tales of a Britain menaced at home by the blowback from dubious foreign deeds are models of Great Power paranoia that resonate today, while Robert Louis Stevenson's romances, which helped "sell" the idea of empire as a thrilling boys' adventure, have been schoolroom staples for a century. Finally, Isak Dinesen's *Out of Africa,* which was brought to a new generation as a film in the 1980s, shows the British takeover of Kenya as a gentle, humorous, romantic affair, played against a backdrop of fabulous scenery.

And yet all of these writers who have been so instrumental in popularizing the imperial agenda of power and dominance were themselves deeply scarred, and as adults bolstered their fragile emotional states through fantasies of empire. Though their experiences may seem extreme, their childhoods are not so different from those of many Victorians. In fact, British Empire was full of individuals who used the opportunities of dominion to compensate for past losses, so full that, Ronald Hyam writes, "it is possible to see a basic truth in the saying, 'love's loss was empire's gain'" (49).[1]

This study of the imperial fantasies of five popular writers of empire will take into account not only the youthful experiences of these writers, but also attitudes toward child rearing during the British imperial period. These attitudes will be read with the help of psychoanalytic theorists who study the connection between childhood experiences and the psychic needs of adults. I draw primarily on the work of Heinz Kohut, considered a leading authority on narcissism since the 1960s. I also draw upon the work of object relations theorists of the 1940s, D. W. Winnicott and W. R. D. Fairbairn, who were pioneers in thinking about the role of relationships in mental health. And I use the work of Alice Miller for her particular emphasis on narcissistic parenting. All of these thinkers, in their different ways, share a sense that failure to support a child's developing identity can result in a famished, divided self.

De Quincey, Stevenson, Kipling, Conan Doyle and Dinesen are similar in that all spin fantasies of deep psychic need in real and imagined imperial environments where the dominant Europeans are free from the usual moral and societal constraints upon adult behavior. All these writers, through their literary renditions of these fantasies, provide models for the psychic uses of empire that were seized upon by their reading publics. And yet, all of those who fantasize empire do so in a way that is peculiarly their own, responding to a particular set of psychic needs. Thus, in the mid 19th century, Thomas De Quincey's literary castigations of all things Asian and his support for the Opium War are linked both to deaths in his family – which, through a small child's irrational magical thinking, were associated with Asia – and to the adult sensation that the Chinese were attacking him continually through the opium to which he was addicted. Somewhat later, Robert Louis Stevenson, who, as a child, was drenched in Calvinist guilt and hysterical hypochondria, would search for a sense of inner freedom, goodness and power, by creating adult characters who could enjoy the happy amorality of infant grandiosity through adventures played out in exotic settings. This vision of infantile perfection, however – along with Stevenson's popularity – could not survive his attempt to live out his dreams in the South Seas.

Rudyard Kipling, the writer most identified with imperialistic jingoism, first, surprisingly, portrayed empire in India as a muddle of bored and sometimes desperate young men, a place where very little is accomplished. Only later in life, as old psychic wounds were re-opened, would Kipling identify whole-heartedly with imperial grandiosity. Around the same time Arthur Conan Doyle, born into a precarious childhood setting of poverty, madness and fantasized greatness, yearned to make a name as the writer of historical romances. Instead, he grudgingly became one of the most famous men in England for his Sherlock Holmes stories, which paint a much more complex picture of the mood of Imperial Britain than do his clichéd and propagandistic histories. Written at the demand of his public, which refused to let the great detective be killed off, these stories portray both the immense appeal of imperial dominance and also a guilty, fearful underside that must be battled but can never be fully repressed.

Finally, Karen Blixen, writing under the pen name Isak Dinesen, portrays her six-thousand acre coffee farm as a feudal estate, and casts the Africans who serve her as loyal, often comical, retainers; to herself she grants the noble status for which she had always yearned, both in her native Denmark and in British East Africa, where she identified with the British aristocrats who had been drawn there by the offer of immense acreages. Paradoxically, the Africans, who are cast as serfs to her great lady, are also given the role of unconditionally loving parents to Blixen's bereft child; in a final role, they are seen as nature's aristocrats, possessed of a natural "right" to existence which she herself lacks.

Since I began to work on this project, the specter of 21st century America as a new imperial power has increasingly been raised, making timely Heinz Kohut's distinction between the "mature aggression" of those rationally fighting a dangerous external foe, on the one hand, and on the other, the irrational rage of those who are compelled to seek revenge for narcissistic injury. I hope that my study of the psyche of imperial Britain may provide lessons and warnings about the motivations for our own aggressions. I also hope that this demonstration of the link between childhood's unfulfilled psychic needs and the desire to dominate others may cause us to look to our children and consider the world they will build.

ACKNOWLEDGMENTS

I would first like to acknowledge West Indian author Jamaica Kincaid, whose works suggested to me to the connection between narcissistic injury and the desire for imperial dominance.

I must also especially thank Clarisse Zimra and Marshall Alcorn for their insightful, thoughtful readings, excellent advice and generous support.

Nora Eisenberg gave valuable thoughts and direction; I am also grateful for points raised by my colleagues at City University of New York–Borough of Manhattan Community College, Joyce Harte, Dexter Jeffries and Ruth Mischeloff. Thanks also to Jeff Kinkley for his thoughts on De Quincey and China, and to the editors of the volume *Masquerades: Disguise in Literature in English from the Middle Ages to the Present* for allowing me the opportunity to explore the idea of aristocratic masking in Isak Dinesen.

The research for this book was generously supported by several Professional Staff Congress–City University of New York Research Grants, the City University of New York Faculty Publications Program, and also by a Borough of Manhattan Community College Faculty Development Grant. My thanks to John Montanez for his help with grant applications.

Grateful acknowledgement is made to the following journals for publishing portions of this research in earlier form: *The Psychoanalytic Review*; *PsyArt: An Online Journal for the Psychological Study of the Arts*; *Connecticut Review*; *scrutiny 2*; *The Journal for the Psychoanalysis of Culture and Society*; and *Psychology of the Self Online*.

Many thanks to Barbara Salz for her invaluable assistance with photo research. Thanks also to the curators of the New York Public Library Berg Collection.

As always thanks to my husband, Burt Kimmelman, for his encouragement and support.

The Narcissism of Empire

Loss, Rage and Revenge
in Thomas De Quincey,
Robert Louis Stevenson,
Arthur Conan Doyle,
Rudyard Kipling
and Isak Dinesen

1   Loss, Rage and Revenge

The Narcissist's Needs

"The mere impressionistic comparison of a nation's familial imagery with her national and international attitudes can easily become absurd. It seems to lead to the implication that one could change international attitudes by doctoring a nation's family patterns. Yet nations change only when their total reality changes." ERIK ERIKSON

The modern portrait of narcissism – a grandiose sense of superiority alternating with feelings of loss, rage and revenge – gives us a model for thinking about imperial relationships. Subject peoples could be of immense psychic use to their conquerors, as they could be compelled in a variety of ways to reflect back to the imperialist a grandiose self-image. These peoples could be made to bow to military or economic force. They could be made to marvel at displays of pomp and brilliance. And through educational systems, which painted the British as godlike, their island home as a green heaven, and their queen as a shimmering fairy, subjects could sometimes be made to believe the British self-portrait of near-magical superiority.[1] Further, relationships with these subjects provided rich opportunities for expressing feelings of contempt, ridicule and revulsion, allowing the imperialist to displace onto others his own feelings of shame and self-contempt.

It must be insisted upon immediately that to consider the psychological satisfactions of empire is in no way to deny the numerous material, social and political motivations of imperial expansion. Empire may not have been as generally profitable as some hoped; Jose Harris claims that in the end empire brought "little profit to the British people at large" and produced a "global balance sheet" that was "in the reverse direction." However, "select" individuals were provided with "innumerable outlets for employment, enterprise, adventure, status and prestige" (5). Further, as Britain in the 1880s lost its undisputed leadership in industry, empire allowed it to maintain the status of capital market of the world, and to be the world's largest trading and carrying nation until 1914. Imperial activities allowed Britain to compete with the newly powerful nations of Prussia and the United States for markets and territory. At home, it was believed that empire had the simultaneous benefit of relieving the country of social pressure, and of rescuing English working men from "poverty, ignorance, drink and exploitation by greedy overseers" through worthwhile work overseas (Girouard 222).

Surely all of these motivations drove the imperial project. An awareness of these material realities, however, should not cause us to ignore the way in which psychological needs color our activities. I do not claim that narcissistic fantasy caused imperial expansion, but that such attitudes helped shape the understanding of the imperial role, so that finally empire was seen not merely as an advantageous economic, social and political arrangement but also as the glamorous, heroic and self-defining mission of a superior people. Even among those not profiting economically from imperialism, historian Eric Hobsbawm writes, the project was genuinely popular since the "idea of superiority to, and domination over, a world of dark skins in remote places was genuinely popular" (70).

Nurture and Narcissism

Before turning to the theories of narcissism developed by Heinz Kohut and a discussion of the relationship of narcissistic needs to desires for dominance, I will consider the views of W. R. D. Fairbairn and D. W. Winnicott, both object relations theorists of the British Independent School of the 1940s. These thinkers did not, like Kohut, focus on narcissism. However, their pioneering study in the psychic harm that can be done when parenting fails makes them important precursors to Kohut.

In moving away from classical Freudian theory and the belief that infants are driven by sexual and aggressive impulses, Fairbairn and Winnicott built upon the work of Melanie Klein and her vision of an infant "wired for human interaction" (Mitchell 113). Though Klein retained Freudian terminology, Stephen Mitchell and Margaret Black write, "her understanding of the basic stuff of mind had shifted, from impulses to relationships, leading to a very different view of the underlying dramas of mental life" (92). For Freud, the aim of the impulse was discharge; the object of desire was the accidentally discovered means to that end. But for Klein, "the object of desire was implicit in the experience of desire itself" (91). According to Judith Hughes, Klein considered external objects – other people, or parts of a person such as a breast or penis – as "psychologically and not simply biologically significant from birth onward" (50).

In Klein's view an infant "introjects" or incorporates into itself an "inner world" of good and bad objects "which is felt by the individual, in deep layers of the unconscious, to be concretely inside himself" (Klein, *Love* 362). The introjection of a "bad object," Klein believed, is driven by the infant's own innate aggression deriving from a death instinct. Because the infant projects its own aggression onto the mother's breast, Klein held, the breast that is introjected is, in part, bad: hateful, poisoning, abandoning. The infant also intojects a "good breast" which is felt to be protective and nurturing.[2]

While Fairbairn and Winnicott broke with Klein's view of an innate aggression derived from a death instinct, they built on Klein's vision of a world of internalized objects. By the mid 1940s Fairbairn was abandoning Freudian ideas about motivation that dominated psychoanalytic theory of the time. Fairbairn concluded that humans were driven not by sexual and aggressive desires as Freudians held but rather by the desire for "human interaction," that is, for love. "Frustration of [a child's] desire to be loved as a person," he wrote, "and to have his love accepted is the greatest trauma a child can experience" (39). What really needed investigating, he believed, was not infantile sexuality, as the Freudians thought, but the relationship between child and caretakers in both external and internal reality.

Children who have responsive parenting, Fairbairn believed, are for the most part healthily oriented toward real human relationships, and less inclined to read all new encounters as reflections of childhood experience. But children whose experience with their parent is frustrating, disappointing or characterized by loss, try to hold onto their parents somehow by internalizing aspects of the "bad" parent. Fairbairn came to see this through his work with troubled children: "At one time," he writes, "it fell to my lot to examine quite a large number of delinquent children from homes which the most casual observer would recognize as 'bad' in the crudest sense – homes, for example, in which drunkenness, quarrelling, and physical violence reign supreme. It is only in the rarest instances . . . that I can recall such a child being induced to admit, far less volunteer, that his parents were bad objects. It is obvious, therefore, that in these cases the child's bad objects had been internalized and repressed." While no child would admit that the parents were bad, Fairbairn found, all of the children readily admitted that they themselves were bad: "It becomes obvious, therefore, that the child would rather be bad himself than have bad objects; and accordingly we have some justification for surmising that one of his motives in becoming bad is to make his objects 'good'" (64–65).

This willingness to internalize even negative aspects of the parent, Fairbairn believed, shows that a child's need for the parent is so great that it seems better to the child to hold onto a bad parent than to feel that he or she has no parent at all: "If a child's parents are bad objects, he cannot reject them, even if they do not force themselves upon him; for he cannot do without them" (67).[3]

The result of such internalization is that the child may become in part like the "unresponsive" aspects of the parent, adopting such features as depression, a tendency toward isolation, or the desire to bully. Fairbairn viewed such internalization as a "splitting" of the ego, with part directed toward the external world, part toward the internalized aspects of the parent. Such internalization can later affect adult life as individuals tend to view new situations in terms of patterns experienced in the earliest relationships.

It is not only children raised in palpably "bad" homes who internalize negative aspects of the parent, however. Since virtually all parenting is flawed, Fairbairn believed, internalized aspects of the parent are present "in the minds of all of us at the deeper levels." The degree to which such internalization results in social or mental ill health depends on a number of factors, such as the "degree of badness" of the experience, and the extent of the child's defenses against negative experiences (65).

Like Fairbairn, D. W. Winnicott also worked with delinquent children. But, as a pediatrician before becoming a psychoanalyst, Winnicott also saw thousands of mothers and babies during the 1940s, so that he entered psychoanalysis with his observations of "mothers and children always before him" (Hughes 128).

A central concept of Winnicott's thinking is that of the "good-enough mother," by which he means a mother who has an early heightened sensitivity to the signals her infant sends. This allows her "to provide almost exactly what the infant needs in the way of holding and in the provision of an environment generally" (Winnicott "Theory" 594). This "good enough mothering," in aiding and reflecting but not overwhelming the child in its perceived needs, affirms the validity of its perceptions, and allows the formation of an "authentic" self: "When there is a mother-infant couple in good working order," he writes, "the infant's ego is very strong. . . . It is this infant, whose ego is strong *because of the mother's ego support,* that early becomes himself or herself, really and truly. . . . It is the well-cared-for babies who quickly establish themselves as persons, each different from any other infant that ever was, whereas the babies who receive inadequate or pathological ego support tend to be alike in patterns of behavior (restless, suspicious, apathetic, inhibited, compliant)" (*Family* 17, italics his).

However, sometimes the caregiver, rather than reflecting the infant's perceptions back to it, requires the child to focus on the caregiver's own needs and perceptions. In this case, the child may be obstructed in responding to the demands of his or her own emerging physical and emotional self. In such situations, "the infant becomes a collection of reactions to impingement, and the true self of the infant fails to form or becomes hidden behind a false self" (*Family* 17). The alternative to being is reacting, Winnicott writes, "and reacting interrupts being and annihilates it. Being and annihilation are the two alternatives" ("Theory" 590).

Heinz Kohut also believed that the responses of the parent play a key role in forming a child's healthy psychological self, so that, Allen Siegel writes, the parent "provides missing psychic functions" for the child who inevitably moves from her infant sense that she is the center of the universe to the gradual acceptance that others exist with a similar set of needs and motivations (36).[4] Every infant, according to Kohut, is born into a normal, healthy state of narcissism, believing that the world revolves around her, indeed, at the beginning, *is* her. This healthy infantile narcissism is one that a good parent supports, reflecting back to the child the sense of her own perfection and importance.[5] Eventually and with the proper care, the infant moves from primary narcissism to healthy selfhood as she matures and faces at age-appropriate times the fact that she is not the perfect center of the world. If the collision of external reality with the child's instinctual wishes is lovingly mediated by a caregiver, Kohut believed, the demands of the infant narcissist within all of us "become gradually integrated into the web of our ego as a healthy enjoyment of our own activities and successes and as an adaptively useful sense of disappointment tinged with anger and shame over our failures and shortcomings" ("Forms" 70).

It is appropriate, Kohut believed, to hold a positive view of ourselves, to experience real self-love, to admire our heroes. We need not deny our ambitions, "our will to dominate, . . . to shine, and our yearning to merge into omnipotent figures." But to live rationally in a world that is not viewed as simply an extension of ourselves, we must learn to transform these desires into "realistic self-esteem."

Kohut paints a hopeful picture of the development of the human child, one driven not by demands for pleasure or tension reduction, as is the Freudian infant, but rather by the desire for connection with others who can both reflect the child's sense of inner goodness back to her, and who can, as needed, embody this goodness. Properly cared for, children can carry into adulthood the sense that they, others, and life itself are good, despite disappointments. "However grave the blows may be to which the child's grandiosity is exposed by the realities of life," Kohut writes, "the proud smile of the parents will keep alive a bit of the original omnipotence, to be retained as the nucleus of the self-confidence and inner security about one's worth that sustain the healthy person throughout life. And the same holds true with regard to our ideals. However great our disappointments as we discover the weaknesses and limitations of our idealized selfobects of early life,[6] their self-confidence as they carried us when we were babies, their security when they allowed us to merge our anxious selves with their tranquility – via their calm voices or the close-ness of their relaxed bodies when they held us – will be retained by us as the nucleus of the strength of our leading ideals and of the calmness we experience as we live our life under the guidance of inner goals" ("Disorders" 183).

But not all children are reared in the sort of supportive environment envisioned here and no child is raised in a perfect environment. The result is that virtually everyone suffers some degree of narcissistic injury, and can be occasionally subject to grandiose fantasy, as well as the "fragmentation" or distraction that occurs "in all of us when our self-esteem has been taxed for prolonged periods" ("Disorders" 185). More serious narcissistic injury occurs when there is a prolonged lack of responsiveness to the child, so that there is little support for the emerg-ing self and little assistance in modifying infant grandiosity. In this case, the grandiose fantasies of infantile perfection and power may be driven into repression, and the adult ego may "tend to vacillate between an irrational estimation of self on one hand and feelings of inferiority" on the other (Kohut "Forms" 69). The resulting narcissism is not, as is often assumed, a condition of self-satisfaction or self-admiration; it is, rather, a condition of deprivation, producing a personality desperate to find others who will nourish it, constantly dreading an attack that will puncture grandiosity. Such personalities need constant self-display and dominance over others to ward off persistent feelings of vulnerability and worthlessness.

Such fears can translate into a deep-seated and compulsive desire for revenge. Often those with narcissistic disturbance were physically or psychologically mistreated as children, and, in "sadistic re-enactments" of their own mistreatment, they will later attack others in a spirit of revenge, even though those attacked may have played no part in the orig-inal injury. Such misplaced retaliation, Kohut writes, is marked by its "utter disregard for reasonable limitations" and by "a boundless wish to redress injury." While this wish is often irrational, "reasoning capacity, while totally under the domination and in the service of the overriding emotion, is often not only intact but sharpened." Kohut likens this feature of narcissistic rage to that of a group of rational technicians carrying out with efficiency the will of a paranoid leader ("Thoughts" 639–40).

Another particular aspect of the rage of the narcissist is that the oppo-nent who has called forth the rage is not seen as separate from the narcissist's self, but instead as a "flaw in a narcissistically perceived reality." The enemy is seen as a "recalcitrant part of an expanded self over which the narcissistically vulnerable person had expected to exercise full control." The narcissist is thus unable to view the enemy, however wrong, as being in some sense like the narcissist himself, a person with particular goals and aims. Rather, the fact that the other person is "independent or different is experienced as offensive by those with intense narcissistic needs" (644).

While Kohut is considered a leading theorist of narcissism,[7] Alice Miller, with books such as *The Drama of the Gifted Child*, originally published in German as *Prisoners of Childhood,* has drawn upon the work of Kohut, Winnicott, and others to focus on the role of narcissistic caregivers. If there is a narcissistic disturbance in a child, Miller argues, it is often the result of narcissistic disturbance in parents or caregivers who have not themselves been appropriately mirrored by a parental figure, and who, rather than responding to the legitimate needs of their children, are themselves "in need of narcissistic supplies," intent upon seeing their favored self-image mirrored in their child. Such people often do not signal that they love and glory in the child for his or her own innate perfection, but link their approval to attainments or accomplishments which reflect favorably upon themselves. Thus these parents require that the child be concerned with the parents' own needs, rather than encouraging the child to develop a separate subjectivity. The child, rather than learning to experience "*his* feelings and *his* emotions . . . develops something which the mother needs, and which certainly saves his life (the mother's love) at the time, but nevertheless may prevent him, throughout life from becoming himself" ("Depression" 326). While the narcissistically damaged child often develops intellectual capacities that support him in his defense against a sense of inner emptiness, narcissistic disturbance may exist untouched behind the façade of intellectual brilliance (328).

Miller sees the narcissist developing two opposing, constantly alternating attitudes: narcissistic grandiosity and, its underside, depression. Behind a depressive mood, there are often unconscious fantasies of grandiosity: "In fact grandiosity is the defense against depression and depression is the defense against the real pain over the loss of the self" (328). The grandiose person, then, must constantly find those who can be made to admire and esteem him, is "constantly occupied body and soul with gaining this admiration" (329). The need is intense, for without it he is in danger of plunging into a depression which requires him to re-experience the loss of self. The narcissist is, thus, powerfully dependent upon those whose admiration and esteem he can compel, though he never feels that he really has enough, for, as Miller writes, "admiration is not the same thing as love" (330)

Depression can occur in the narcissist when grandiosity breaks down as a result of failure or even illness, for these setbacks can temporarily interfere with his effort to continually perform his perfection. While "continuous outstanding achievements" can "maintain the illusion of constant attention and availability of his self-object," he must keep delivering brilliant performances to ward off feelings of loss. And even brilliant success can lead, after the initial flush wears off, to depression, for success only masks childhood frustrations, and "can only bring momentary satiation" (Miller 332–33).

Such a person, for whom life is lived as a defense against a breakthrough of feelings of loss and emptiness, is also trapped in what Miller calls "the vicious circle of contempt." Often such a person has been the object of contempt by a narcissistic parent or caregiver and in adulthood is contemptuous of others since contempt is "the best defense against a breakthrough of one's own feelings of helplessness." The healthy person, by contrast, knows and to some extent accepts his or her own weakness, and "does not need to demonstrate strength through such contempt" (*Drama* 67).

Narcissism and Victorian Childhood

All of these thinkers show that empathic parenting is essential to the development of a healthy sense of self. Without such support, Kohut and Miller believe, children may suffer narcissistic injury and be subject to feelings of contempt, irrational rage, grandiose fantasies of dominance, and the depression that strikes when grandiosity is punctured. When we look at the childhood of the Victorian upper middle class, however, we see that children were virtually never raised by their parents, but rather were turned over to caretakers whose chief focus was the externals of a child's life, not the validation and mediation of a developing subjectivity.

Though the Victorians did not take care of their own children, they were still very interested in childhood. While they did not "discover" it, as has sometimes been claimed, they were fascinated by it, Claudia Nelson writes, perhaps in part due to the demographics of the time; in the period between 1851 and 1881, children under fifteen made up approximately thirty-five percent of the population of Britain and Wales (69). Despite a general interest in education and child development, the misery-filled lives of children found in many Victorian *bildungsromans,* as well as the stories found in Victorian autobiography, paint a picture of neglect and an adult world unable to "fathom childish needs." The charge that adult incomprehension could "prove lethal, even to children of wealthy, aristocratic, and normally conscientious adults" was made with frequency (79). Charles Dickens, for example, paints dozens of children whose emotional needs are of no interest to adult caretakers. "I was not actively ill-used," David Copperfield confides, of his treatment at the hands of the Murdstones:

> I was not beaten or starved, but the wrong that was done to me had no intervals of relenting, and was done in a systematic, passionless manner. Day after day, week after week, month after month, I was coldly neglected. I wonder sometimes, when I think of it, what they would have done if I had

been taken with an illness, whether I should have lain down in my lonely room, and languished through it in my usual solitary way, or whether anybody would have helped me out. (157)

Often, Steven Mintz writes, children were viewed as the property of their parents or guardians, to whom they owed duty and obedience, and children in many homes were placed under an "enormous burden of expectation" (13). Tyrannical and despotic fathers are often encountered in the memoirs of the period, and Samuel Butler's account of a childhood with a "ceremonially sadistic" father and a mother who "manipulates love and emotion" is only an extreme example (Mintz 45). In fiction, too, children labored under a burden of debt to parents and guardians. The orphan Jane Eyre, for example, is taught that she must never forget the "obligation" she owes her aunt for saving her from the poor house and must accept unfair treatment as a result of her "dependence" (Bronte 44). In Dickens' *Dombey and Son*, the well-to-do father views his children as adjunct to his own needs, effectively murdering his son in the effort to turn him into the heir he desires.

The charge of adult neglect and incomprehension is made so frequently in Victorian literature, Nelson writes, that later decades saw a "backlash in the form of sugary magazine fiction about intensely loving relationships between golden haired moppets and old men who, like Silas Marner, flattened to unidimensionality, devote their lives to surrogate fatherhood." However, such sentimental accounts continue to show that adults were primarily interested in children for services they could provide. In this case children function as a kind of "spiritual palate cleanser – a dose of innocence and purity protecting adult men, in particular from the moral dubiousness of the public sphere" (Nelson 79)

The high incidence of emotional neglect of children, or the view that children were possessions whose inner life was of little importance, may have been a result of the fact that well-to-do parents rarely saw their children, and when they did their relations were marked by formality, rigid discipline and distance (Harris 85). In many Victorian homes middle class children saw their parents only at morning prayers, and between five and six in the evening. The actual duties of child rearing were seen as matters for specialists, the nanny and other servants with whom the children spent the rest of their time. These caregivers were not necessarily trained to their work, Nelson observes, but were professionals in the sense that they were paid to care for children full time. Even when children were with their parents, Penny Kane says, their access was conditional, as servants were always available to step-in and take away a troublesome child (39).

Since children were raised mainly by servants, the nurse or nanny was often the real authority in the child's life. Marion Lochhead writes, "in many a family it was she who ruled, who made laws and decisions; who decreed tacitly the times when parents and other adults might visit 'her' nursery and when 'her' nurslings might go downstairs" (9).

This influential figure found her place in a society that had long been in the habit of allowing others to raise its children, according to Jonathan Gathorne-Hardy. In the fifteenth century an Italian observer noted that "the want of affection in the English is strongly manifested towards their children" as at the age of seven they are put out "to hard service in the houses of other people, binding them generally for another seven or nine years." The thinking behind this practice, which was seen even in wealthy families, was the medieval idea that it was necessary to learn "to serve others before you could lead" or even live among others (34).

In the 18th century, though parents played a larger role in their children's lives than they would in the next century, contact between children and mother could be quite limited and children still might see a parent for only one hour a day. Jane Austen's niece remembered that, "Children were kept in the nursery out of the way not only of visitors, but of their parents; they were trusted to hired attendants, they were given a great deal of exercise, were kept on plain food, forced to give way to the comfort of others, accustomed to be overlooked, slightly regarded, considered of trifling importance" (qtd. in Gathorne-Hardy 61).

Then, in the 19th century, a set of social circumstances contributed to the virtual professionalization of childcare for the upper classes. Medicine improved and the rate of infant mortality was down. With the Industrial Revolution a great deal of wealth was created and concentrated in the hands of a relative few who could afford to hire servants for almost every purpose. Meanwhile, the great numbers of unemployed poor were eager to take jobs in service (66). These economic circumstances and the class assumptions they bred meant that in the 19th century and early 20th century "it is inconceivable that upper class mothers would have looked after their children" (Gathorne-Hardy 314).

There were undoubtedly many devoted and loving servants; surely some nurtured children better than parents might have done. Winston Churchill's nanny, Mrs. Everest, for example, is cited as one who provided the confidence and security of "strong and continuous love" (Gathorne-Hardy 32). Still, employment depended not upon the ability to truly love and to wisely guide a child's inner development, but to feed, clothe and discipline. Not surprisingly, there are many reports of servants who failed utterly to step into the role of the caring, involved parent, a role which is seen by Kohut and others as necessary in helping a child develop a stable sense of self and mediate primary narcissism. Some nannies seem to have been unable to resist the temptation to use their small charges for their own "covert emotional relief," to use Erik Erikson's term. "Too often," Gathorne-Hardy writes, "one is driven to the conclusion that Nannies vented upon their little children, under the guise of discipline, not spoiling

George Nathaniel, Marquess Curzon as Viceroy of India. Known for his bullying of subordinates and his routine humiliation of Indians, Curzon as a child was tyrannized by his nanny whom he described as "brutal and vindictive." In addition to beating the boy, locking him in dark cupboards, and tying him up for long periods in uncomfortable positions, Curzon's nanny also dealt in shame, once forcing him to write a letter to the butler asking for a birch so that he could be punished for lying. The letter was to be read out in the servants' hall.

and the rest, emotions generated by their dissatisfied, frustrated, neurotic or downright sadistic temperaments" (275).

One child with such a nanny was the young Lord Curzon, who became a man of ambition and arrogance who rose to great heights in imperial Britain but who died "embittered, frustrated and unsatisfied." In unpublished papers Curzon wrote of his nanny, as "a brutal and vindictive tyrant. . . . She persecuted and beat us in the most cruel way and established over us a system of terrorism so complete that not one of us ever mustered the courage to walk upstairs to tell our father or mother. She spanked us with the sole of her slipper on the bare back, beat us with brushes, tied us up for long hours to chairs in uncomfortable positions with our hands holding a pole or a blackboard behind our backs, shut us up in darkness." In addition to corporal punishment, Curzon's nanny dealt in shame, once making him write a letter to the butler asking for a birch with which he was to be punished for lying and "requesting him to read it out in the servants' hall" (Gathorne-Hardy 302–3). The tormented child would, as an adult, himself be accused of sadism during his years as Viceroy of India from 1898–1905: "It is evident," Denis Judd writes, "that Curzon was easily hurt and also enjoyed hurting others." He was cruel to his mistress, and "bullied his subordinates so constantly that when he left India it was said that there was not a single administrator of any standing whom he had not personally insulted; he routinely humiliated Indians, even the princes he affected to admire" (176).

Other nannies were not necessarily cruel but gained power by making "everything as unpleasant, uncomfortable and frustrating as possible." The conditions in the upper class nursery, Gathorne-Hardy writes, "the restrictions, the severity, the deprivation and instability" are so "reminiscent of the home backgrounds of delinquents that one wonders why they weren't all criminals" (276, 290).

Children seldom told of their experiences with nannies, believing, as some of the accounts he cites show, that their treatment was simply a fact of life. And the most ferocious nanny could "retire into a background of obsequious gentility" when a parent would visit the nursery (281). Still, Gathorne-Hardy says, "one can't help feeling [parents] should have found out more. . . . No Englishman or woman at any time during our period would have dreamt of employing anyone untrained or unintelligent to look after their horses, yet time and again fools or sadists or incompetents were allowed to bring up children" (281).[8]

All five of the writers I examined were raised by adults whose near-fanatical religious views led to the belief that children were inherently evil and in need of constant correction and punishment, much of which would be considered abusive by today's standards. Their childhoods do not seem to have been particularly exceptional, however, as during the Victorian period, both parents and servants were likely to subscribe to the idea of

THE WILLOUGHBY CAPTAINS.

By TALBOT BAINES REED,

Author of "The Fifth Form at St. Dominic's," "My Friend Smith," etc.

CHAPTER XXVI.—AN EXPLOSION OF "SKY-ROCKETS."

PARSON, Bosher, King, and the other Parrett's juniors were in bad spirits. It was not so much the Rockshire match that was preying on the brotherhood, grievous as that blow had been. Nor were they at the present suffering under any particular infliction, or smarting under any special sense of injustice. Their healths and digestions were all tolerably good, and the mutual friendship in which they had been wont to rejoice showed no signs of immediate dissolution.

School bullies from a story in an 1884 *Boys' Own Journal*. Well-to-do boys as young as six were sent to boarding schools which prided themselves on a system of self-governance, which meant that most authority over younger boys was delegated to older boys who were free to tyrannize their juniors. The situation of the younger boys was sometimes described as "slavery," as "hard and as barbarous as the treatment of negroes in Virginia."

innate evil, derived from the Puritan movement of the late 16th century (Marshall 20). Despite the views of Jean-Jacques Rousseau that children were born in a state of purity and that it was the role of the parent to nurture the child's inborn benevolence, the Puritan attitude is most frequently reflected in Victorian child rearing advice. It would follow from this view that the grandiosity of a child's primary narcissism was something to be crushed, often with physical punishment, and that caregivers would be little inclined to "reflect [the infant's] own sense of infantile perfection back to him," as Kohut advises. Rather, Peter Marshall writes, the child's will was to be broken; and books on child development suggested that caregivers "inflict bodily pain so steadily and so invariably that disobedience and suffering shall be indissolubly connected in the mind of the child" (24). Not only should evil be beaten out of children, but parents were also advised to regiment a child's life within a few months of birth, and to avoid sentimentality such as kissing or rocking, as these gestures would be taken by children as "a sign of weakness" that could retard the development of respect for authority (29).

Finally, there were many British boys, such as De Quincey, Kipling and Conan Doyle, who were brought up, at least in part, by other children at a boarding school. Boys from the age of six were sent to such schools, many of which prided themselves on their system of "self-governance." This meant that most authority over younger boys was delegated to older boys, who were sometimes benevolent, but who were also free to tyrannize their juniors until the younger boys were old enough to take their turn at tyranny. Typically boys of all ages were locked up at night in huge dormitory rooms and left without supervision until morning. The men who passed through this system could differ about its "benefits and injuries," John Chandos writes, "but on the point of its hardship nobody disagreed." It was, one alumnus reported, "as hard, and as barbarous as the treatment of the negroes in Virginia" (87). Indeed, the situation of the younger boys is often described as that of "slavery." One former ruling senior boy wrote, "Slavery warps the character of both slave and master, and slavery is the only word which summed up the three years of experience of a college junior. Its details, whether cruel or grotesque, were all so contrived as to stamp upon the young boy's mind his grade of servile inferiority and his dedication to the single virtue of abject and unquestioning obedience" (89).

For little boys, yet to be formed by the self-governance system, the trauma could be intense. Suicide and death were not infrequent. "Children torn away from mothers and sisters [at the age of six] not infrequently die," Thomas de Quincey writes. "The complaint is not entered by the registrar as grief; but *that* it is. Grief of that sort, and at that age, has killed more than ever have been counted amongst its martyrs" ("Suspiria" 148).

Though some parents – mothers and fathers alike – undoubtedly shuddered at the idea of sending their little boys to such a life, most were convinced that it was the best way – in the modern world, the only way, for a boy to become a man and a gentleman. There appears to be in this attitude an extreme fear of softness and weakness, so much so that the brutalization of little children seems a preferable alternative: "I grant the system of education is bad," Lord William Russell wrote in a letter to a kinsman about plans for the education of an only son. "A boy learns little and there are many objections to a public school – but it fits a boy to be a man . . . it is an essential part of our constitution and makes our patricians so superior to those of the continent. . . . I wish you could see how a young Roman nobleman is brought up – you would not wonder at him turning out the being he is" (qtd. in Chandos 26). Once parents sent children to school, they were not expected to take much notice of them, and children appear to have had little encouragement or opportunity to complain. Letters home were examined and corrected by teachers, as these missives were viewed primarily as a means to "shed credit on the school, rather than as a means of communicating and strengthening family bonds" (Kane 38).

It seems clear that such a system of child rearing would contribute to narcissistic disturbance as theorized by Kohut; not only were small children denigrated and brutalized by older boys, but masters also used physical punishment as a way of making their students work. Such practices seem tailor-made for driving the normal, grandiose fantasies of childhood into repression, thwarting the "legitimate" needs of children to be "understood, taken seriously and respected" as well as their ability to mediate primary narcissism into a mature acceptance of self and others.

But the school experience was pervasive among the middle and upper classes, and it was formative for many key figures of empire: "Old –school-tie loyalties, clubland fellowship and gang fraternities seem to have been almost a more important emotional prop than marriage," Ronald Hyam writes. "Many members of the ruling elite seem to have suffered degrees of emotional retardation – those who never got over being head prefect at school" (46). Though the public school was designed to make men of boys, the men of empire admired "boyishness," and "many of the great men of the Empire were essentially boy-men" who had "never been able to outgrow their boyhood ideals" (47).[9]

Such a school system, Jonathan Rutherford writes, often had the effect of creating men who were perpetual adolescents. Torn from thoughtful adult nurture too soon they "could never fully repress the trauma of maternal loss." The story *Peter Pan*, by J. M. Barrie, first performed to immense acclaim in 1904, is a story of "lost boys" who yearn for a mother and who are determined never to grow up. It was, Rutherford writes, "the culminating adventure story of the Victorian era and revealed what had been repressed and denied in the imperial fantasy of manly, racial supremacy – the domestic world of mothers, sexuality and emotional need" (25).

The case is sometimes made that widely-practiced childrearing methods are, by virtue of their general use, "normal" or "natural." But Erik Erikson argues that what everybody does isn't necessarily "natural," and that northern European practices are not necessarily the norm worldwide or throughout history. He notes, for example, that in the 19th century American Plains Indians were shocked at the physical and psychic brutality with which the whites treated their own offspring: "It takes a particular view of man's place on this earth, and of the place of childhood within man's total scheme to invent devices for terrifying children into submission, either by magic, or by mental and corporeal terror. . . . It is clear that the concept of children as property opens the door to . . . misalliances of impulsivity and compulsivity, of arbitrariness and moral logic, of brutality and haughtiness, which makes men crueler and more licentious than creatures not fired with the divine spark" (*Young* 69).

Shared Grandiosity / Shared Loss

Given some of the attitudes toward childhood in the Victorian era, it is not surprising that characteristics of narcissistic injury – an un-integrated grandiosity, a parasitic use of others, irrational rage and desire for revenge, contempt, and an underlying sense of vulnerability – are exhibited in varying degrees by many individuals during this period. While everyone, certainly, was not raised under such extreme conditions as the subjects of my study, the experience was far from uncommon.

Certainly not everyone in England supported the imperial project and many were repelled by the jingoism into which the country plunged at moments of crisis, but even these seem to have recognized that they were rowing against the tide. "The whole country has gone mad . . . with the lust of fighting glory," Wilfrid Scawen Blunt wrote in his *Diaries* in 1898, when British and French interests clashed in Fashoda in the Sudan, "and there is no moral sense left in England to which to appeal" (Porter *Critics* 58).

The Boer War occasioned "a flood of propaganda against 'capitalist imperialism' never equaled in England subsequently," Porter writes, but "little came out of it in the way of a policy toward the colonies. . . . On the one side there was this imperialism with its un-blushing self-assertiveness and its mass-emotional appeal; on the other a notoriously divided Liberal Party, liable to break into fragments at the very mention of the word empire, its leaders soft-pedaling and saying nothing on vital imperial issues" (*Critics* 64, 70). In private, Sir Henry Campbell-Bannerman, the leader of the Liberal Party, was "repelled" by the "jingo 'flag-waving' and imperialistic 'Cock-a-doodle do,' and by the depraved national temper which these years manifested." But, Campbell-Bannerman generally kept these opinions to himself: "Jingoism was too strong, it seemed, to be reasoned with. As an irrational emotion it made all discussion on rational grounds irrelevant and unnecessary. . . . Imperialism was not merely, or even chiefly, a colonial policy; it was a national psychology" (76, 90).

And of course not everyone who has narcissistic fantasies sought dominance in empire. Then as now there are other ways to seek the sense of superiority that the narcissist craves. Still, it is clear that imperialism would offer particular benefits. In service of the imperial project, one could join with others with whom one shared both grandiosity and a secret sense of emptiness and loss, thus making the condition seem quite normal. For, Kohut writes, there are groups that are held together by this "shared grandiose self." When "acceptable" outlets for approval or prestige are blocked, groups, like individuals, may react with the sort of aggression which takes on "overtly and covertly, the flavor of narcissistic rage in either its acute or, even more ominously, its chronic form" ("Thoughts" 658).

It is impossible to trace with certainty the link between individual upbringings and larger social movements. But some theorists see a connection between the human psyche and the actions of people in society. W. R. D. Fairbairn claims that in societies in which immature individuals predominate, the tendency to "treat others as objects or things" will be enhanced (xvi). And in her study of prejudices, Elisabeth Young-Bruehl suggests a connection between the personal and the social, arguing that groups may share the same underlying fantasies. "Especially in moments of crisis," she argues, "a dominating set of social character traits may emerge, affecting the whole society;" those who possess such "dominative" character types will have "more chance to flourish, to organize groups, to gain power, and to exercise influence" (342).

Finally, Erikson, in his discussion of German youth before World War II, provides an example of the relationship that can exist between individual lives and group movements. In his essay, "The Legend of Hitler's Childhood," he examines the authoritarian German father whose harshness lacked "true inner authority," and masked a sense of drift after the dislocations of the First World War. But harshness without inner authority "breeds bitterness, fear and vindictiveness," and Erikson believed the lack of firm patriarchal figures led young people to look for some other form of belief, in "the adherence to some mystic-romantic entity," a search that ended for many with Hitler's Third Reich (*Childhood* 332, 335).

Imperial Pessimism / Imperial Triumphalism

As the nineteenth century progressed, the story the British told about themselves became both "evangelical and self-justifying," (Druce 189) with those engaged in imperial work portrayed as saviors to their colonized subjects. The 1849 remarks of William Kingston, a committee member of the Society for Promoting Colonization, were echoed in hundreds of popular publications and productions. The British, he declared, had been "awarded the office" of peopling the globe and "spreading the arts of civilization, and more than all, of promulgating the true faith of Christ among the lands of the heathen" (qtd. in Druce 189.) Children, in particular, were inculcated in the civilizing mission of empire through hundreds of magazines and history books extolling the "peace and civilization which it was the glory of British statesmen" to bring to the "backward nations of the earth" (Castle 12). The sense of the virtue of the British imperial mission was underpinned by history lessons, which emphasized the "conflict, romance and heroism of the British past" (Castle 5). "There is little doubt," Kathryn Castle writes, "that the sheer volume and invasive nature of imperial propaganda directed at the rising generation did help to shape images of self, and certainly of the 'others'" (4).

One aspect of the grandiose self-image created by the British during the imperial period was the vision of an exalted mythic past, a portrayal which allowed them to envision imperialism and the domination of others as one more episode in a uniquely glorious history. As John M. MacKenzie says, a "perverted" form of medieval chivalry had, by the late 19th century, become a part of the "British imperial cult" as "heroes from both the distant and more recent past were assiduously promoted through children's literature" (3). So pervasive was this glorification of medieval England that it may seem to us now to have always been a part of English life. Yet the creation of an inflated and grandiose national tradition based on tales of chivalry was quite new, Mark Girouard writes; in the rationalist 18th century, the British had little use for the old stories of chivalric quests, finding them "barbarous and absurd," (18) an attitude that may have had a good deal of basis in reality as "all too often medieval knights were brutal, quarrelsome and self seeking" (16). In the 19th century, however, there was a great upsurge of interest in medieval England; as confidence in empire faltered, the self-mythologizing became increasingly grandiose. It was, says John Mackenzie, quoting economist John Hobson, a time of "hero-worship and sensational glory, adventure and the sporting spirit; current history falsified in coarse flaring colors" (49). If the imperial mission was viewed as a crusade at home, there was, Lewis Wurgaft writes, a great deal of magical thinking on the ground in India that ran counter to sober doctrines of administrative order as the exercise of what felt like unlimited power was "almost sensually experienced" (59).

Yet, the final decades of the century were also a time of "growing self doubt and cultural panic" in Britain as "expressions of anxiety about social regression and national decline were widespread" (Boehmer 33). Images of "disease and contagion," Anne McClintock writes, reached "into almost every nook and cranny of Victorian social life" (46), and feelings of national insecurity were "at least partly at the root of much jingoistic exaltation and triumphalism" (Judd 139). The uncertainty, Hobsbawm writes, was "double edged." If empire was vulnerable to its subjects, "though perhaps not yet," was it not more immediately vulnerable to "erosion from within of the will to rule. . . . Would not the very wealth and luxury which power and enterprise had brought weaken the fibres of those muscles whose constant efforts were necessary to maintain it? Did not empire lead to parasitism at the centre and to the eventual triumph of the barbarians?" (43).

"Whitewash" and Other Concerns: Problems with Psychoanalytic Theory

In the course of writing this book, I have learned that to undertake such a study is to present oneself as a sort of Rorschach test of attitudes about psychoanalytic theory and its use in literary and cultural studies, and I would like to discuss some of these attitudes before going on.

One of the most important concerns that has been raised is that a psychoanalytic examination of imperialist figures is a form of "whitewash," a bid to excuse crimes on the basis of childhood woes, a disgraceful attempt to cite a few tears in an upper-class nursery as an excuse for actions that have resulted in the devastation of millions. To consider this serious charge, it is helpful to examine the controversy between Italian psychiatrist Octavo Mannoni and Martinican Marxist Aimé Césaire.

Mannoni was one of the first to read imperial conquest as an act of psychological weakness rather than strength, claiming in his 1950 book, *Prospero and Caliban: The Psychology of Colonization*, that the colonist, far from acting out of strength, is motivated by a profound sense of loss. "No one becomes a real colonial," Mannoni writes, "who is not impelled by infantile complexes which were not properly resolved in adolescence" (104). Further, he argues, no one who finds himself in the colonies stays long if not driven by psychological needs: "A person free from complexes . . . would not taste those emotional satisfactions which, whether consciously or unconsciously, so powerfully attract the predestined colonial" (98).

In his portrait of Europeans who are drawn to imperial power, Mannoni looks back at the development of Western culture in general, and specifically the drive to relinquish ancestral gods and traditions and family structures in the name of individualism and rationalism. He sees that, unlike peoples bound to more traditional ways, the modernized Westerner is an "orphan," cut off from sustaining belief or kinship systems, "trying clumsily to behave like a grownup" (56). The "complexes" which Mannoni observes in these figures in his Freudian reading cause the colonial both to project onto his subjects his own perceived faults, weaknesses and fears, and at the same time to identify with these subjects as he searches to revisit some perceived lost paradise. The latter desire, Mannoni writes, "casts doubt upon the merit of the very civilization [the colonial] is trying to transmit" (21). Part of the lure of imperialism, Mannoni claims, is that it allows one to leave one's surroundings for a world in which the reality of other human beings does not intrude upon one's fantasies, where one sees others in terms of one's subjective needs, where, like Peter Pan, one need never grow up. However, "If we are to achieve a complete and adult personality, it is essential that we should make the images of the unconscious tally, more or less with real people; flight into solitude shows that we have failed to do so" (101).

While Mannoni does not deny the material advantages of imperialism, he does not see them as necessarily central, claiming that the imperialist often sacrifices profit for the sake of other, psychological, satisfactions. Mannoni's views anticipate Albert Memmi, who, in 1957 would write that while there are some Europeans who cannot stomach the colonial setting and who return to Europe, there are others, the "mediocrities," who remain to paint a suspiciously "too magnificent portrait" of imperial power (Memmi 48, 58). Similarly, Memmi claims that the shrewd, profit-oriented businessman is seldom found in the colonies: "The best go away." Why? "It is a bad sign to decide to spend life in the colonies, just as it is a negative indication to marry a dowry" (46).

Mannoni's argument, that imperial power is driven by an inner emptiness rather than strength, is also supported by Frantz Fanon in *Black Skin, White Mask*. Though Fanon objects to several of Mannoni's views, such as the claim that colonized peoples are more willing to accept dependency than Europeans, he approves of the "intensity . . . with which M. Mannoni makes us feel the ill-resolved conflicts that seem to be at the root of the colonial vocation" (107.)

Mannoni's dissection of the emptiness at the heart of the imperial project would not seem to put him in the imperialist camp, but would rather make him a critic of imperial motives, and one who undermines attitudes of superiority. However, as a result of a furious attack upon his work made by Césaire, Mannoni is often remembered today primarily as a white apologist for the subjugation of people of color. For Césaire, Mannoni's description of the Western man's "orphaned" state, as opposed to the Madasgascans' "dependence" upon family and traditional culture, is just another way of repeating "the old refrain: 'The Negroes-are-big-children.'" In an outraged response, Césaire indicts Mannoni's analysis of imperialism and by implication the analysis of white writers generally: "They take it, they dress it up for you, tangle it up for you. The result is Mannoni. Once again, be reassured! At the start of the journey it may seem a bit difficult, but once you get there you'll see, you will find all your baggage again. Nothing will be missing, not even the famous *white man's burden*" (40, italics his).

The use of psychoanalytic theory is portrayed here as a slick way to take familiar racist beliefs, whitewash them, and restate them in a way more palatable to a post-World War II Western world, a world in which the gleam of European imperialism had become tarnished and where, following the Nazi holocaust, racist attitudes that were too overt had become distasteful: "Away with racism! Away with colonialism!" Césaire writes. "They smack of too much of barbarism. M. Mannoni has something better: psychoanalysis. Embellished with existentialism, it gives astonishing results: the most down-at-heel clichés are resoled for you and made good as new; the most absurd prejudices are explained and justi-fied" (40).

Finally, Césaire sees Mannoni's psychoanalyzing of imperialism as part of a "persistent bourgeois attempt to reduce the most human problems to comfortable hollow notions." To give a psychological reading of imperi-alism is only the first step, Césaire writes, toward "absolving" its "blood-thirsty" perpetuators (42) and continuing the business of material domination as usual. "What has become of the Banque d'Indochine in all that? And the Banque de Madagascar? And the bullwhip? And the taxes? And the handful of rice to the Madagascan or the *nhaque* [a pejorative name given by the French to people of Indochina]? And the martyrs? And the innocent people murdered? And the bloodstained money piling up in your coffers, gentleman? They have evaporated! Disappeared, intermin-gled, become unrecognizable in the realm of pale ratiocinations" (43).

Before persisting with a psychological reading of imperialism, it seems important to consider the motivations and effects implied by Césaire. The first question I would like to consider is whether a psychological exami-nation of imperialism necessarily vitiates attempts to acknowledge and correct material inequity. In Césaire's impassioned language one can feel the disgust at those who would ponder psychological theories when people don't have enough to eat, a sense that it is asinine to even speak of a psychic "lost paradise" experienced by those who are busy dominating and enslaving others. Rather than pondering the psychology of imperial-ists, we should, Césaire's Marxist-influenced argument indicates, focus all of our energies upon changing economic and political realities.

Ironically, however, Césaire's Marxist rejection of a psychological reading of imperialism mirrors attitudes held during the post World War

II period by the Western capitalist establishment, which has also resisted looking into the psyche for the roots of the desire to dominate. Here too racism and colonial domination are usually seen as ills deriving from "nationalist politics and colonial history, from capitalist greed and mass unemployment, and from poverty and global uncertainty," as Christopher Lane writes in *The Psychoanalysis of Race*. In the post-war period, Marxists and members of the Western establishment alike believed that change in material and political realities would wipe out attitudes of racial superiority, and the desire for dominance. This belief betrays, Lane suggests, a "foundational hope" that humans, given the chance, just want to get along if material needs can be met. Repeatedly, however, this belief, finally held by Marxists and capitalists alike, is not born out, and we find ourselves forced to take note of an unpleasant "psychological truth" that not all gains are tangible: "For instance, a group's 'gain' might consist in the pleasure received in depleting another's freedom . . . if we ignore these psychic issues, we promulgate fables about human nature, maintaining idealistic assumptions while unexamined psychic factors fuel acrimony, resentment and hatred" (Lane 5).

The argument summarized above allows us a response to Césaire. It seems undeniable that particular theories of human subjectivity can contribute to a people's continued oppression, while simultaneously allowing the oppressor to deny guilt; the zeal of Christian missionaries, who served as a vanguard for imperialism in many parts of the world, might be offered as an example of this. But the claim that consciousness is determined by material reality is *also* a theory of human subjectivity, and may itself be used to contribute to oppression, meanwhile denying the oppressor's guilt, as has been demonstrated by events in the twentieth- and twenty-first centuries, in communist and capitalist countries alike. The point, I think, is that virtually any theory of human subjectivity can be used as a tool of oppression, whether that theory be grounded in Christianity, Islam, Enlightenment rationalism, Marxism, capitalism, or psychoanalysis. Rather than ruling out a particular theory, we should examine its usefulness while staying alert to the motives behind its use.

Despite Césaire's attack, Mannoni's idea of the inner emptiness of imperialism has been re-visited recently by some post-colonial writers and scholars. Kenyan novelist and political journalist Ngugi wa Thiong'o has portrayed the English in his country as displaced persons, alienated from home and god, sustained only by their ability to dominate others (*Weep* 76). West Indian writer Jamaica Kincaid has described the imperialist as one who may have "fashioned for himself a body of steel," but whose hard shell conceals an interior that is dead and decaying (76). Sara Suleri writes that literature of empire "reorganizes the materiality of colonialism into a narrative of perpetual longing and perpetual loss (10) as the British feel "culturally overpowered" in a setting as diverse as India (19). And

Elleke Boehmer shows that even as the European imperialist rejects the native "he also requires the native's presence in order to experience to the full his own being" (64). The politics of race, Homi Bhabha has written, "will not be entirely contained within the humanist myth of man or economic necessity or historical progress, for its psychic affects question such forms of determinism" (61).

Finally, though she is writing about the portrayal of "Africanist" figures in American literature, Toni Morrison, in her critical work, *Playing in the Dark*, provides a powerful incentive for examining the use white writers make of their characters of color, and for considering what this use teaches us about the psychology of racism and domination. While it is important to look at what oppression does to the mind and imagination of the oppressed, Morrison writes, "equally valuable is a serious intellectual effort to see what racial ideology does to the imagination and behavior of masters" (12). In a discussion of Willa Cather's *Sapphira and the Slave Girl*, for example, Morrison shows that Cather uses the relationships she sets up between white and black characters to "dream and redream" her "problematic relationship with her own mother" (27). For, Morrison writes, "the subject of the dream is the dreamer. The fabrication of an Africanist persona is reflexive; an extraordinary meditation on the self; a powerful exploration of fears and desires that reside in the writerly conscious" (17).

Another concern that might be expressed about a study such as mine is that it once again privileges a Western world view. And while we should be on guard that we do not consciously or unconsciously accept self-serving or false cultural attitudes, we should also take care to avoid an equally great ill: the subtle tendency found in most responses to trauma to blame the victim rather than the perpetrator, to seek, in Judith Herman's words, "an explanation for the perpetrator's crimes in the character of the victim" (116). It is of course necessary for post-colonial studies to listen to the voices of imperial subjects. But while these subjects have much to tell us about imperialism, it is not their responsibility to explain its creation. The place to seek an explanation for the acts of empire must lie in the character of the imperialist, and this is what psychoanalytic theory will help us probe.

Other critics of my approach may include feminists who fear that by examining the relationship of childrearing to empire, I seek to blame all the ills of the world on women. I understand that, theoretically, women in Victorian England were given the responsibility for the moral and spiritual well-being of those whose domestic sphere it was their vocation to oversee (Ellis 70). In practice, however, this role was only theoretical, as the child's life was usually turned over to servants and boarding schools.

Further, women could not have been expected to fight a system of childrearing that was approved by everyone around them. There is evidence that even the most loving of mothers supported often harrowing childcare arrangements since they, along with the rest of society, believed these were for the child's ultimate good. *In Boys Together: English Public Schools 1800–1864*, for example, John Chandos cites letters written by a boy named Milnes Gaskell, newly arrived at Eton, to his mother: "You have no idea how savage the boys are," he writes. He hears "the must brutal species of swearing in existence" and wonders what is the use of doing his lessons since older boys take them from him under threat of flogging. The accounts of this "cruel new world" surely troubled Mrs. Gaskell, who we know "was a most loving and solicitous mother," Chandos writes. "But there is no suggestion anywhere in the letters that she responded, or that Milnes expected her to respond, either by removing him from school, or by applying to the headmaster for redress or mitigation of his grievances. She had probably learned enough from her own brothers and her husband to know that the latter was beyond the power of the headmaster, while as for the former it would have been a betrayal of the faith . . . that the experience of public school education would prove in the end the best training for what was expected of him in life that of an English gentleman could receive. Her conduct is consistent with the attitudes of other mothers of her class and her time to the sufferings at school of their sons" (66–67). In the pages that follow, we will see that the emotional nurture of children is misunderstood or neglected as much by fathers, guardians, servants and school officials as by mothers in a pattern so widespread and so widely accepted as to make it impossible to assign blame to any one group.

For some, psychoanalytic theory itself may be inherently suspect. There are those, perhaps, who fear being dragged into contemplation of their own formative experiences. (Indeed, this may be a view that intellectuals are particularly prone to, as intellectualization is a well-known psychological defense against failures in emotional nurture.) Or, it may be as Kohut says, citing Freud, "everybody tends to react to psychoanalysis as a narcissistic injury because it gives the lie to our conviction that we are in full control of our mind" ("Thoughts" 645).

Others understand psychological inquiry as the tiresome quest of whiners to blame all their troubles on childhood grievances. But of course this view is itself "psychology." As Erikson has commented, almost all of those who undertake to explain human actions are engaged in "psychology" whether they admit it or not. Those who are opposed to "systematic psychological interpretations permit themselves the most extensive psychologizing – which they can afford to believe is common sense only because they disclaim a defined psychological viewpoint. Yet there is always an implicit psychology behind the explicit anti-psychology" (*Young* 35).

Another problem with the use of object relations theory and Kohut's work on narcissism is that the ideas of French psychoanalyst Jacques Lacan have long filled much of the space allotted to psychoanalytic theory in literary and cultural studies. Lacan and Freud are so frequently the only theorists cited that it sometimes appears their views *are* psychoanalytic theory. There are, to be sure, notable exceptions. Jeffrey Berman's *Narcissism and the Novel* provides an overview of the concept of narcissism as developed by Freud and object relations theorists Heinz Kohut and Otto Kernberg, before turning to an analysis of character in the novel. Marshall Alcorn's *Narcissism and the Literary Libido* uses the work of Kohut and others to examine the way texts may interact with readers' own narcissistic needs. Barbara Johnson uses Kohut to read Nella Larsen's *Quicksand*, a work Johnson describes as one of "racial double consciousness."[10] Catherine Rising has used Heinz Kohut to read Conrad, while Judith Kegan has drawn upon his ideas to advance feminist theory.

Despite these significant exceptions, the fact remains that Lacan is the psychoanalytic theorist most frequently cited, and Lacanian readings of every imaginable aspect of literature abound. Lacan's theories seem useful, many people agree, in that they provide interesting metaphors for experiences of loss and alienation. One can see how one of Lacan's most well-known notions, that of the "mirror" stage of human development, works particularly well as a metaphor for the exchanges of racism and imperialism, as this image portrays a human subject which is formed from the outside by alienating images.

While Lacan's writing is subject to varied interpretations, the mirror stage theory is generally read as one which posits an ego that is built upon outer illusions, symbolized by the self that is not quite the real self the child sees in the mirror. As a result the self is finally always alienated from itself. In Lacan's words, "The mirror stage is a drama whose internal thrust is precipitated from insufficiency to anticipation – and which manufactures for the subject, caught up in the lure of spatial identification, the succession of fantasies that extends from a fragmented body-image to a form of its totality that I shall call orthopedic – and, lastly, to the assumption of the armour of an alienating identity, which will mark with its rigid structure the subject's entire mental development" (4).

Though he does not refer directly to racism or imperialism in his mirror stage essay, Lacan does refer to the events of World War II where, perhaps for the first time, Europeans could imagine themselves as the victims of an experience already well-known to many non-European peoples, subjection to the physical and psychological dominance of a brutal and well-organized occupier.

The problem with Lacan's theory of the formation of the alienated subject is that there is little evidence for it, and a great deal of evidence to the contrary. Lacan sees narcissism as the "irreducible and atemporal condition of human reality," Jeffrey Berman contends. But he "offers remarkably little clinical material to support his psychoanalytical episte-mology," dismissing "any attempt empirically to validate this psychoanalytic theory or integrate it with general psychology" (29). And Norman Holland, in his essay, "The Trouble(s) with Lacan," says that "there is no evidence whatsoever for Lacan's notion of the mirror stage." There is, he writes, no evidence that the child makes a judgment that the mirror image "is unified or in some sense more powerful or otherwise different from the self. . . . What the child is finding out is that the image in fact reflects the self." Holland notes that Lacan's idea of the split and self-alienated self is modeled on the outmoded linguistics of Ferdinand de Saussure, which divides language into *langue*, a formal system of signs, and *parole*, people's actual speaking. "I cannot think of a serious psycholinguist who would agree with Saussure's or Lacan's account of the way we understand language," Holland writes.

> Indeed, today's cognitive science shows the opposite. Words do not simply imprint meanings on our minds as Saussure thought. Words require consid-erable processing. . . . Any elementary textbook in the psychology of reading or the psychology of language would make this clear. The only justification for Saussure's and Lacan's idea that signifiers impose them-selves on persons is the apparently compelling need of some intellectuals to feel that the individual is not autonomous. Their account is simply and unequivocally false by today's standards.

The Lacanian idea of the human subject created by alienating images is also refuted by contemporary studies with infants. These studies, some of which are discussed in Daniel Stern's *The Interpersonal World of the Infant*, describe an infantile "core-self" which is organized around an "experiential sense of events" such as the authorship of one's own actions, the ability to decide to move a hand or a foot, for example. Sense of self is not, Stern writes, "a cognitive construct. It is an experiential integra-tion. This sense of core self will be the foundation for all the more elaborate senses of the self to be added later" (71).

And while Lacan's theory assumes an unfulfilled desire for the mother, Stern's discussion of research with children shows that at a very early age infants are aware of being in a complex relationship with an attuned care-giver, a relationship in which one is both known and knowing. "By nine months," Stern writes, "infants have some sense that they can have a particular attentional focus, that mother can also have a particular atten-tional focus, that these two mental states can be similar or not, and that if they are not, they can be brought into alignment and shared" (130).

While I welcome illuminating metaphor, I would argue for a distinc-tion between theories that are useful philosophically or metaphorically, and those which are based on clinical study that may help us better under-stand the actual development of human subjectivity. As Daniel Dervin has said, "As long as [Lacan's] verbal performances dazzle and stimulate us to new possibilities of encountering texts, or to unconventional lines of inquiry, we are enriched. But if we press his metonymies and metaphors too closely we can expect disappointment" (139).

Then there is the concern that the use of psychoanalytic theory leads to an argument that is "reductive." For, as David Hunt notes, psychoanalysis *is* a reductionist science, "attempting to find the laws of personality, the uniformity of human behavior beneath the façade of individual and cultural differences" (4). But while it is appropriate to be suspicious of a too-totalizing use of any doctrine – whether that be a particular psychoanalytic theory or even the notion of "indeterminacy" – I would argue that we hobble ourselves in trying to study questions of real-world importance if we surround inquiry with too many taboos. When we talk about imperial dominance, we are talking about attitudes and actions that have diminished – and continue to diminish – the lives of millions. As Anne McClintock warns in *Imperial Leather*, postcolonial criticism remains a "formalist" exercise "unless one also undertakes the more demanding historical task of interrogating the social practices, economic conditions and psychoanalytic dynamics that motivate and constrain human desire, action and power" (73).

And Elisabeth Young-Bruehl, in her psychoanalytic study, *The Anatomy of Prejudices*, takes up the doctrine of indeterminacy as she discusses the claim that the Nazi holocaust can't be narrated through traditional historical modes. Those who make such claims, she maintains, are influenced by the current academic "fad for trying to write in a postmodernist style that avoids supposedly naïve modernist claims to truth and verifiability. The sincerity of this 'problematizing' seems questionable when it is affectless and intellectualized and when authors show themselves caught up unthinkingly in dilemmas of anti-Semitism" (463). Similarly, I would argue, we should struggle not to allow hidden attitudes that may result from our own continued participation in Western dominance to lurk in the recesses of "indeterminacy."

If writing is, as Marshall Alcorn has claimed, a "socially shared imaginative space," then, let us now consider what we can learn about the shared imagination of empire by examining, with the help of object relations theory, the fantasies of some of its most widely-read and best-loved writers.

2 | THOMAS DE QUINCEY

Dreams of China

"In China . . . I am terrified by the modes of life, by the manners, and the barrier of utter abhorrence, and want of sympathy, placed between us by feelings deeper than I can analyze. I could sooner live with lunatics or brute animals." THOMAS DE QUINCEY

In 1822, twenty-five years before Freud was born, and long before he formulated his theory that dreams contain secrets of human subjectivity, Thomas de Quincey began writing about his own dreams, showing them to be a window on a turbulent inner life accessible in no other way. And more than a hundred years before the psychoanalytic theorists showed that a breakdown in emotional connections between infant and caregiver could result in depression and retarded emotional development, De Quincey wrote about the ongoing role played by childhood mistreatment in the emotional lives of adults.

To be sure, in a time when a great deal of harsh treatment of children is accepted as a matter of course and is even seen as a strengthening tonic, De Quincey is quick to express his own disdain for those who would be un-English enough to seek sympathy or understanding for their emotional suffering. "English feelings," he writes on the first page of *Confessions of an English Opium Eater*, are "revolted" by the "spectacle of a human being obtruding on our notice his moral ulcers or scars." Leave such confessions, he advises, to "adventurers, or swindlers," or to "the spurious and defective sensibility of the French" ("Confessions" 1).[1]

His own "confessions," he explains, are delivered primarily that others may benefit from his experience with opium, which he has indulged in "to an excess not yet *recorded* of any other man" (2). Despite De Quincey's disclaimers, however "Confessions" focuses almost entirely upon the author's emotional "scars," his ongoing sense of abandonment, and his attempt to comfort himself with the drug.

Similarly, "Suspiria de Profundus," written twenty-two years later, opens with the claim that the purpose of the book is informative, to reveal the way in which opium allows users to experience the "grandeur" of human dreams. This is a concern, De Quincey writes, in an era when the press of modern life renders many people too busy and too lacking in solitude to dream (88). Though the stated theme is an explanation of the "dream faculty," the work, again, revolves primarily around events of De Quincey's childhood. Midway, the author seems to realize how far he has strayed from his purported subject and tries to connect the two topics logically: "The nursery experience had been the ally and the natural co-efficient of the opium," he reflects. "For that reason it was that the nursery experience had been narrated. Logically, it bears the very same relation to the convulsions of the dreaming faculty as opium" (137).

Despite his own prejudices against those who examine their "moral ulcers," De Quincey develops in these pre-psychoanalytic times a complex reading of the human subconscious, describing the human brain as a "palimpsest" where the "tragedies of infancy" remain, "lurking below all, and . . . to the last" ("Suspiria" 146). In addition to probing the layers of his emotional life through dreams and replaying scenes from youthful tragedies, De Quincey also, unconsciously, reveals his inner emotional landscape in his writings about Asia. In his autobiographical works, as well as in his prolific journalism about the conflict between England and China that would result in the Opium War, De Quincey obsessively replays scenarios of loss, injustice and humiliation in Oriental settings. These seem to derive from several sources: childhood exposure to both Bible stories and the *Arabian Nights*, his infant connection between death and Oriental climates, and his subjugation to the Asian drug, opium.

Though he has insights into the workings of the human consciousness, De Quincey does not pretend to understand fully the connection between the inner life of the child and that of the adult. He never makes a direct link between his childhood losses and the ongoing depression that makes the temporary bliss derived from opium so irresistible. Nor does he find in his own psyche the source of his fantasies about Asia or of his obsession with the Chinese, whose humanity he denies and for whose destruction during the Opium War he furiously and irrationally lobbies. However, an examination of De Quincey's writing may allow us to make some of these connections, to link his childhood to his opium use, and to his project of demonstrating the sub-human nature of the Chinese. His writing may also, unwittingly, help us form a further connection to the psychological attitudes that supported imperialism.

De Quincey's childhood, and the experiences to which he obsessively returns in his writings, can be read as a case study of the sort of narcissistic injury described by Heinz Kohut, Alice Miller, and others. The young Thomas and his siblings were left almost entirely to the care of servants, as his father was away conducting trade in the West Indies most of the boy's life, returning only to die. His mother, as described by Grevel Lindop, was a deeply religious but cold woman who communicated with her household through a housekeeper to make sure distinctions in rank were observed. "Speak to mistress?" one maid is recorded to have remarked, when asked why she had not gone to Mrs. De Quincey with a problem. "Would I speak to a ghost?" (Lindop 8).

Similarly, Mrs. De Quincey's relationships with her children revolved around the concept of "filial duty" rather than affection. When Thomas's older brother, William, was troublesome at the age of five, he was sent away to school. For the children who remained at home she had little patience, and was, De Quincey later wrote, "predisposed to think ill of all causes that required many words." In an age when people revered their parents as a matter of course, De Quincey wrote of his mother carefully: "If I could presume to descry a fault in my mother, it was that she turned the chilling aspects of her . . . character too exclusively upon those whom, in any degree, she knew or supposed to be promoters of evil. Sometimes her austerity might even seem unjust" (Lindop 7). Of Mrs. De Quincey (originally Quincey; she added the "De" when Thomas was a teenager), Edward Sackville West wrote, "It is abundantly clear that . . . although an attentive mother [she] inspired more irritation than love in her children." And he notes that two of her four sons ran away from home (4). It may be indicative of Mrs. De Quincey's outlook that when her son Richard returned to England after years at sea but refused to see his mother, she quickly came to the conclusion that since he would not see her, he could not be her son, and declared the man to be an impostor intent on perpetrating a scam.

Without father or loving mother, Thomas was forced to look for support from servants and siblings. With the latter, he had good fortune, reveling for a time in the love of his two slightly older sisters, Jane and Elizabeth. He was especially dependent upon Elizabeth, who acted as a gentle mother to her smaller brother (Lindop 8). When Thomas was four and a half years old, however, the younger sister, Jane, died, and in "Suspiria de Profundis," he reports that his first thought was that she had been treated harshly by the servant in whose charge she was, betraying an early sense of children harmed by those who are supposed to care for them. "The feeling I had upon me was a shuddering awe, as upon a first glimpse of the truth that I was in a world of evil and strife" (98).

Then an even more horrible blow struck, one which would be, De Quincey's later writing reveals, a defining event of his life. When the boy was seven, Elizabeth too died. Her death occurred in bright summer weather, and, as described in "Suspiria de Profundis," the boy crept into the room where her body lay. The contrast between the extinction of the only source of love and tenderness in his life and the brilliant summer day outside the open windows triggered a profound and lasting association between Elizabeth's death and another heart-rending death the boy had learned of, the death of Christ. Like Elizabeth, Christ too died in "summer," the warm oriental climate, as a nurse had once explained while reading a Bible story, of the Holy Lands. This connection between the death of what is most beloved and hot, summer-like Asian climes, where the fact of death appears to be mocked by a "tropical redundancy of life" ("Suspiria" 103), will come to dominate De Quincey's fantasies. This linking of death and the East will appear to contribute to his later irrational execration of all things Asian.[2]

In "Suspiria de Profundis," De Quincey portrays his childish self as totally bereft after the loss of Elizabeth: "Deep is the solitude in life of millions upon millions who, with hearts welling forth love, have none to love them. Deep is the solitude of those who, with secret griefs, have none to pity them. . . . But deeper than the deepest of these solitudes is that which broods over childhood" (114). The thought of suicide was immediate: "Should we go to *them*?" (120). There appears to have been no one to comfort the child in his loss. The boy in "Suspiria" was sent to the funeral in a carriage with men he didn't know. They were kind to him, but soon begin talking of ordinary matters, a conversation that was "a torment" to the distraught child (108). Someone, possibly a servant, possibly his brother William, who was brought home for the funeral, mocked him for his grief and told him to cease his "girlish" tears. But, De Quincey remembers, the word "girlish" had "no sting for me, except as a verbal echo to the one eternal thought of my heart – that a girl was the sweetest thing I, in my short life had known – that a girl it was who had . . . opened to my thirst fountains of pure celestial love, from which, in this world, I was to drink no more" (111). Thenceforth, however, he "wept in secret" (112). When some time later servant girls comforted and kissed him when his kitten was killed, he was afterwards struck that he had received no such comfort when Elizabeth died: "If I had met with so much sympathy, or with any sympathy at all from the servant chiefly connected with myself in the desolating grief I had suffered [over Elizabeth]," he writes, "possibly I would not have been so profoundly shaken" (123). While De Quincey is able to imagine that a servant might have helped him in his grief, the thought that he might have been comforted by his mother seems not to have occurred to him.[3]

But it was not only maternal coldness and the loss of the mother substitute that formed De Quincey's emotional life. After the death of his father when Thomas was seven, his brother William, who was five or six years older, and who had been living in the dog-eat-dog struggle of boarding school almost all of Thomas's life, returned to live at home, and spent the next few years establishing himself as master to Thomas's slave (West 11). The games William invented were designed to highlight his own power as compared with Thomas's weakness and were often played out in an imaginary scenario of conquest in exotic lands. In a time when Britons were voyaging to all corners of the world, William's games were infused with both the thrill of aggression and the horror of the unknown peoples who were encountered. A play written by William was first entitled "Sultan Selim," then changed to "Sultan Amurath," considered "a much fiercer name, more bewhiskered and beturbaned" (Barrell 59). All of the children of the house were required to perform in the play, and their characters were all massacred in the first act by William, who took the title role. For the second act, "a new generation had to be created only to be massacred again, and so on through all the remaining acts" (59).

In another game, the boys invented imaginary kingdoms. Thomas deliberately imagined his own kingdom, Gombroonia, as "underdeveloped and impoverished" in an attempt to "escape the aggressive intentions of William's kingdom, [Tigrosylvania], which was large, expansionist and apparently invincible" (61). Soon it was discovered by William that the Gombroonians were sub-humans and possessors of tails. So great was Thomas's shame at this revelation, Barrell writes, "that he identifies himself and his subjects as helpless outcasts, on a par with pariahs, Jews, gypsies, lepers, the Pelasgi, and the Pyrean Cagots. He and they are all polluted by 'some dreadful guilt, real or imputed,' of which the humiliating Gombroonian tail becomes a symbol" (61). These childhood games, with their focus on the cruel power of the conqueror and the degradation of the conquered, appear to have set the stage for De Quincey's later fantasies of England and China.

Thomas's subjection to his brother, Edward Sackville West writes, was painful, but at the same time "brought him a queer voluptuous delight." As a child will cling to a parental figure, even an abusive one, Thomas seems to have cherished his brother's attentions, even when these reduced him to subhuman status. "I had a perfect craze for being despised," De Quincey later wrote. This brotherly contempt was "a sort of luxury I was in continual fear of losing" (qtd. in West 13). Even this dubious emotional attachment, however, was undone by death, as William, sent off to be an apprentice in London, died of typhus at the age of sixteen.

As Thomas grew older, his relationship with his mother and the guardians who had been appointed by his father revolved around battles over where Thomas was to go to school and how much would be spent; funds were chronically low, due in part to Mrs. De Quincey's various building projects. The boy was intellectually precocious, another common feature of narcissistic damage, Alice Miller writes, as the "intellect assume[s] a supportive function of enormous value" (*Drama* 38). Thomas was enrolled in Bath Grammar school, where he was happy and a star pupil, but his mother took him out, possibly because she was not comfortable with the success Thomas had achieved at school or the praise he received there. De Quincey recounts that the headmaster of the school and some other men called on his mother to tell her of her son's promise and to urge her to return him to school. "It illustrates my mother's moral austerity," De Quincey would later write, "that she was . . . altogether disturbed at what doubtless these gentlemen expected to see received with maternal pride" (qtd. in Lindop 28). Finally, he was sent to Manchester Grammar School where he was bored and depressed. He wanted to change schools, but nothing could be agreed to. His guardians, he believed, were not interested in his well-being, only his "unconditional submission" ("Confessions" 8).

Depressed and desperate, the sixteen-year-old De Quincey, who had no plan or money, ran away. He went first to Wales, where he sometimes managed to lodge with poor families but was forced to sleep out of doors as his funds dwindled. From Wales he made his way to London. Whatever the actual facts of De Quincey's London sojourn, the description he gives of himself and his fellow sufferers in "Confessions" can be read as a portrait of his inner sense of utter destitution and abandonment. Starving, homeless, without friends, money or prospects, he is afraid to contact acquaintances for fear that he will be captured by his guardians. It is one of the ironies of narcissistic damage that the child is most harmed by precisely those who are supposed to nurture him, and in the "Confessions" De Quincey simultaneously shows himself as deeply pitiful, but also as one who does not expect pity.

After several months out of doors, he describes being allowed to sleep on the floor in the upper reaches of a freezing, mostly unfurnished house of a somewhat shady lawyer, whose acquaintance De Quincey seems to have made in a failed attempt to borrow against his expected inheritance. De Quincey does not, in "Confessions," tell the story of Elizabeth's death; that will not come until "Suspiria de Profundis" twenty-two years later. But while it cannot be clear to readers at the time, we can see, given what was later revealed, that De Quincey here revisits his own childhood loss by creating two fellow sufferers, both doomed young girls. These destitute creatures not only replicate Thomas's inner state of abandonment, but also replay the drama of Elizabeth, a sweet loving girl to whom Thomas clings, who is helpless to save him and whom he is helpless to save. Such re-enactment of loss is common, Miller argues, as those with narcissistic damage seek unconsciously to grasp the source of their sadness: "What cannot be recalled," she writes, is "unconsciously reenacted and thus indirectly discovered" (*Drama* 19).

The first girl drawn by De Quincey is a "poor friendless child" of about ten years of age who lives in the near-abandoned house where De Quincey shelters. She is "hunger-bitten" and aged by suffering. He speculates that she may have been the illegitimate child of the lawyer who inhabited part of the house, or she may have been a servant. At any rate, she spends the nights in terrified solitude in the house's dark and cold unfurnished upper rooms: "The house was large; and from the want of furniture, the noise of the rats made a prodigious echoing on the spacious stair-case and hall, and, amidst the real fleshly ills of cold, and, I fear, hunger, the forsaken child had found leisure to suffer still more . . . from the self-created [fear] of ghosts" (16–17). As a young boy, Thomas had sought warmth and protection from his small sisters. Now the teen-aged Thomas and the child huddle together for warmth and "security" against the chill of loss and loneliness that surrounds them: "When I was not more than usually ill, I took her into my arms, so that, in general, she was tolerably warm, and often slept when I could not" (17). But while he can offer the girl his warmth and affection, and while she is a comfort to him, they are powerless truly to help one another: "I promised her protection against all ghosts whatsoever: but, alas! I could offer her no other assistance" (17).

The drama of love and loss between Thomas and his sister Elizabeth is revived in yet another young woman, that of the sixteen-year-old prostitute Ann, whom he tells of meeting as he wanders in London. Like De Quincey, she is "poor and friendless," and like him a "walker of the streets." Like him she is a good, "noble-minded" person who has been treated harshly, her "little property" brutally taken from her (21). Both she and Thomas are children of that "stony-hearted" mother, Oxford Street, "that listenest to the sighs of orphans and drinkest the tears of children" (34). Clearly Ann's destitution and De Quincey's are similar, but she resembles Elizabeth as well. Like Elizabeth, Ann is kind and motherly, full of compassion, "ministering [to his] necessities when all the world had forsaken me" (21). At one point he faints and believes he would have died if Ann had not run to buy "out of her own humble purse" a glass of port which restores him. But she too is taken from him. When he leaves London for a few days in a futile attempt to borrow money, he returns to find her missing from their meeting place, and he never finds her again. His address to her could as well have been made to Elizabeth: "Oh! youthful benefactress! how often in succeeding years, standing in solitary places, and thinking of thee with grief of heart and perfect love, how often have I wished that . . . the benediction of a heart oppressed with gratitude [would have the power] to pursue thee . . . into the darkness of the grave – there to awaken thee with an authentic message of peace and forgiveness and of final reconciliation!" (22).

After a time, Thomas returned to his family and arrangements were made to send him to Oxford, where, he later recalled, he did not in two years utter one hundred words. De Quincey portrays himself during this time as unable to escape the trauma of painful past experience: "Suppose," he writes, that a man has been "suspended by some colossal arm over an unfathomed abyss, suspended, but finally and slowly withdrawn – it is probable that he would not smile for years. That was my case" (qtd. in West 58). To the poet William Wordsworth, whom De

Quincey admired and with whom he had tried to begin a correspondence, he wrote, "I have lived under a perpetual sense of desertion" (qtd. in West 66).

It was at this time that De Quincey, who was suffering from face pains, was prescribed opium, and suddenly discovered, through use of the drug, a sense of well-being previously unknown. Here, he writes, was a "panacea . . . for all human woes: here the secret of happiness . . . happiness might now be bought for a penny, and carried in the waistcoat pocket: portable ecstasies might be had corked up in a pint bottle: and peace of mind could be sent down in gallons by the mail coach" ("Confessions" 39).

De Quincey's language shows that, for him, opium is more than pleasure. Rather, for a time it seems to give him the sense of well-being of which the narcissistically damaged child is too soon deprived. Opium is, he writes, "a healthy restoration to that state which the mind would naturally recover upon the removal of any deep-seated irritation of pain that had disturbed and quarreled with the impulses of a heart originally just and good." If London's harsh Oxford Street represents the "stony-hearted" mother who seems to be nourished by the grief of her children, opium appears in the guise of the good and gentle mother, soothing away fear and pain, comforting the child with the sense of his own rightness, always seeming to "compose what had been agitated, and to concentrate what had been distracted" (41).

But though the drug seems for a time to function as a soothing parent, opium itself will eventually be drawn into the endless cycle of need and abandonment, and the soothing good mother will be transmogrified into a torturing fiend. For eight years, De Quincey claims in *Confession*, he was able to use the drug moderately, but in 1813 he began to take it daily, so that it was like breathing. Undoubtedly he was physically addicted in a way that was not entirely understood at the time. What he felt was that he couldn't face his emotional state without the drug: "I hanker too much after a state of happiness, both for myself and others," he observes. "I cannot face misery."

By this time Thomas had left Oxford and gone to live in a cottage in Grasmere. He declares himself happy, opium still having the effect of rolling away "the cloud of profoundest melancholy" ("Confessions" 55). But an event takes place – or was dreamed, though it is reported as fact – which signals that the Orient, identified in childhood as a site of cruelty where innocents were made to suffer, is now his everyday companion in the form of opium.[4]

The event is the appearance at the door of De Quincey's cottage of a "Malay," a figure in a turban and "loose trowsers," a "tiger cat." That the "Malay" and the vile Orient he represents are the antithesis of innocent and pure English childhood is shown by the juxtaposition De

Quincey makes between him and the young English serving girl who announces that a "demon" has come to the door: "A more striking picture there could not be imagined," De Quincey writes, "than the beautiful English face of the girl, and its exquisite fairness, together with her erect and independent attitude, contrasted with the sallow and bilious skin of the Malay, enameled or veneered with mahogany, by marine air, his small, fierce, restless eyes, thin lips, slavish gestures and adoration." Though the Malay is "slavish" he is simultaneously fearsome, and De Quincey writes into the scene a little child, who is reminiscent of De Quincey's young self looking to his sister for protection. The child timidly "gaze[s] upwards at the turban and the fiery eyes beneath it, whilst with one hand he caught at the dress of the young woman for protection" (56).

The Malay, real or imagined, signals a shift in De Quincey's opium use. The narcissist, Heinz Kohut believed, vacillates between a sense of grandiose perfection, and one of emptiness and loss. And now opium begins to play its role in this scenario. Opium, seen first as the calming good mother, now is transformed into a cruel agent of loss and pain. Through a childhood identification of the Orient with death and degradation, and now through the treachery of the Eastern drug opium, De Quincey has come to connect the East with his inner misery. The personification of this connection in the form of the Malay demonstrates the way in which Asians will provide De Quincey with a socially acceptable, if irrational, outlet for the rage and sadistic desire for revenge which, as Kohut has written, often marks the victim of narcissistic damage. De Quincey was, as have been many people then and now, clearly inhibited in speaking, probably even thinking, of the cruelty and neglect he had experienced at the hands of his mother and other family members and caregivers. Though De Quincey grasps that there is a relationship between childhood misery and adult suffering – "Man is doubtless *one* by some subtle *nexus* that we cannot perceive, extending from the newborn infant to the superannuated dotard" (Suspiria 107 italics his) – psychoanalysis has yet to theorize the connection. But to fear and revile the East would become increasingly acceptable in the mid-nineteenth century, as China resisted British demands for open trading ports and finally sought to cut off the opium trade, upon which Britain relied as a means of paying for indispensable Chinese teas (Fay 120). In his impassioned and lengthy articles in support of the Opium War, De Quincey would find an endless supply of imagery with which to portray his ongoing sense of loss, panic, rage, and psychic doom.

Though De Quincey's obsession with the East is no doubt fanned by the excitement of the Opium War, it is very much in evidence in "Confessions of an English Opium Eater," written years before that conflict. Here the East is already both hideously "other" and horribly familiar. It is the "cradle" where "youth" and "individuality" are crushed

A LITTLE TEA PARTY.

BRITANNIA. "A LITTLE MORE GUNPOWDER, MR. CHINA?"   CHINA. "O—NO—TAN—KE—MUM."

"A Little Tea Party," a cartoon published in *Punch, or the London Charivari* in 1858. Following China's defeat by England in the Opium War in 1842, relations between the two countries were peaceful for a time but in 1856 a new war broke out. These new hostilities sent De Quincey into a frenzy of anti-Chinese journalism and pamphleteering in which he expressed his outrage at the "inhuman insolence of this vilest and silliest among nations." Here a *Punch* cartoon reflects a similar attitude, showing China with its rich clothing and pidgin speech as simultaneously pompous, cowardly and foolish. In a play on words – gunpowder is a type of Chinese green tea – Britannia satirically offers China tea from a gun-shaped teapot.

by the omnipotence of the "ancient" and "cruel," and where humans flourish only in the untended state of a "weed." It is a scene in which the "dim and reverential feelings" due to one's elders are buried beneath the misery they cause. De Quincey's writings about China are voluminous despite the fact, as West has written, that they display a "complete ignorance . . . of Chinese history, and [an] incomprehension of Chinese civilization" (252). De Quincey's opinions of China seem to be informed in part by his nursery fare of Bible stories and tales from the Arabian Nights, but most of all by his own inner emotional landscape, upon which opium has provided garish embellishments. The imagined China becomes the hostile environment in which De Quincey replays his sense of childhood oppression. His first expression of the horrific Asian scenes into which he is delivered by his opium dreams is so telling that I quote at some length from "Confessions of an English Opium Eater."

> The Malay has been a fearful enemy for months. I have been every night, through his means, transported into Asiatic scenes. I know not whether others share in my feelings on this point; but I have often thought that if I were compelled to forgo England, and to live in China, and among Chinese manners and modes of life and scenery, I should go mad. The causes of my horror lie deep; and some of them must be common to others. Southern Asia, in general, is the seat of awful images and associations. As the cradle of the human race, it would alone have a dim and reverential feeling connected with it. But there are other reasons. No man can pretend that the wild, barbarous, and capricious superstitions of Africa, or of savage tribes elsewhere, affect him in the way that he is affected by the ancient, monumental, cruel and elaborate religions of Indostan, &c. The mere antiquity of Asiatic things, of their institutions, histories, modes of faith, &c. is so impressive that to me the vast age of the race and name overpowers the sense of youth in the individual. . . . Man is a weed in these regions. . . . In China, over and above what it has in common with the rest of southern Asia, I am terrified by the modes of life, by the manners, and the barrier of utter abhorrence, and want of sympathy, placed between us by feelings deeper than I can analyze. I could sooner live with lunatics, or brute animals. (72–73)

While the standard attitude of Europeans – including De Quincey in later writings – is that non-Europeans lack real civilization, we see here that it is precisely China's "impressive" and ancient institutions that make her so threatening.

If these dreams link "monumental, cruel, and elaborate" Asia to the adults who appear huge, ancient, and omnipotent to children, they also re-work the connection between tropical Asian climes and the death of innocents. In the opium dreams that De Quincey records in *Confessions*, we see him veering from one side to the other of the narcissist's inner equation of grandiosity on the one hand, and the sense of loss and victimization on the other, revealing what Milligan calls De Quincey's "radical instability of the self" (46), all played out in a fantasy of the Orient. In one dream he goes from being an "idol" and a "priest" who is "worshipped" to a human sacrifice. Like the child who feels himself abandoned and punished for unknown crimes, he is said to be guilty of some horrible but unspecified deed; he is simultaneously kissed "with cancerous kisses," buried alive "for a thousand years, in stone coffins," and abandoned, perhaps like the infant Moses, "laid, confounded with all unutterable slimy things, amongst the reeds and Nilotic mud" (74). That these dreams represent the terrors of the helpless infant is born out, I think, by De Quincey's juxtaposition of his account of them with the sweet voices of his own children who come to his bed to wake him. By this time, De Quincey has married the daughter of a local farmer and begun the family that will eventually number eight children. Here the sweet innocence of his children's voices brings home to him the horror of infancy violated, and with a "mighty and sudden revulsion of mind," he weeps (74).

In another complicated dream, love and joy are smothered in Eastern horror. In this dream, De Quincey perceives himself to be in a tranquil English scene at dawn on Easter Morning. He sees the grave of a child whom he had "tenderly loved" and thinks that on this day of resurrection "old griefs shall be forgotten" and "I will be unhappy no longer." Upon this thought, however, the scene changes to "an Oriental one" where it is also Easter Sunday, and he sees the domes and cupolas of an Asian city, as a "stain" upon the horizon. And there, seated under a palm tree is the lost Ann, the young London prostitute. De Quincey speaks to her but she doesn't reply, and at that moment "vapours" and "thick darkness" come on, and he is back in Oxford Street (76). We see that Easter Sunday, with its hope of resurrection of the dead, of sorrow transformed into joy, cannot withstand its remove to an Eastern clime, where all hope of joy must be transformed into sorrow. Such hope and promise will always be dashed, and one will always be returned to a cold and heartless environment, here represented by "stony-hearted" Oxford street.

In another dream, there is a similar sense of initial hope, this time on a vaguely imperial scale. But here too hope is swamped by inevitable doom, and again there is the loss of beloved female innocents. The dream is begun with strains of the Coronation Anthem, a piece of music written for the coronation of George II. The music suggests vast armies on the march; it is a "mighty day" one of "crisis and final hope for human nature, then suffering some mysterious eclipse, and laboring in some dread extremity" (77). De Quincey himself, as it seems in the dream, would have the power to decide the outcome if he could somehow find the will to act, but he seems to be buried under a paralyzing weight. Then it seems that all is lost, and female forms pass, allowed only a moment of heartbreaking farewell. Once again, the hope that all will be miraculously well is dashed;

once again he has been unable to save beloved young women from destruction.

Though De Quincey will, in fact, be a lifelong opium addict, he concludes the *Confessions* with the claim that he has broken the habit, seeming to recollect, somewhat belatedly, that the stated intention of the work was to explain opium use to the uninitiated. The real effect, though, has been to play and replay the scenario of a paradise lost, the continued yearning for the bliss of tender love, and the inevitable destruction of one's hopes so that one's weakness and helplessness are again revealed. As he closes "Confessions," De Quincey uses an image from Milton. Like Adam and Eve, he can not help gazing back at the gates of Paradise, from which he has been eternally expelled, but however long he may look they are always guarded by devils "with dreadful faces" and "fiery arms" (80).

De Quincey is primarily known today for his "Confessions of an English Opium Eater," first published in 1821, and is thus often seen as a Romantic writer. But most of his essays, which fill the many volumes of his collected writings, were written during the Victorian period as De Quincey struggled, always on the verge of ruin, to support a large family with his pen. In 1840, as the Opium War neared, he published the first of a number of lengthy essays excoriating China, essays in which a near total ignorance of the actual Chinese co-existed with the certainty that the Chinese had not the slightest right to question the English incursion into their country, or England's decision to flood China with opium, despite long-standing Chinese protests (West 252). Although there were those in England who opposed the Opium War – Nigel Leask calls it the only episode of Imperial history "that is generally seen as unambiguously wicked" (217) – De Quincey was of course not alone in his support or in the corresponding derision of the Chinese. But his screeds against the Chinese are marked by the intensity of their emotion, and also by the way in which the Chinese, in his hands, continually slide from a stance of cruel and arrogant omniscience to one of laughable weakness. The imaginary Chinese, I believe, are cast in two roles. First they refigure De Quincey's powerful mother, guardians, and brother. Second, they are cast as the young Thomas himself, weak and "girlish," contemptibly helpless. In this second role, China appears to have become Thomas's ridiculous imaginary kingdom of subhumans, Gombroonia, created by William to reflect glory upon his own kingdom of Tigrosylvania. By creating the Chinese as weak and even sub-human creatures whom he may despise, De Quincey undertakes the characteristic revenge of the narcissist as described by Kohut, re-enacting his own mistreatment, this time with himself as oppressor rather than oppressed.

In two lengthy articles, "The Opium Question with China in 1840," and "China," written in 1857, De Quincey shows China first of all as a bully. In a way that suggests the child's secret view of his domineering but relatively dull-witted brother William, and also of his mother and guardians, China is shown as having no real strength or virtue, no legitimate beliefs or claims, but to prevail simply through its sheer immensity. "China was great," he writes, "in pure virtue of her bigness" (231). And though always taking care to exalt Britain, De Quincey still betrays the sense of Britain's vulnerability as compared to the immense "tonnage" of China. China, he writes, is defensible, "without effort of her men, by her measurable extent, combined with the fact of having no vulnerable organs" ("Opium" 177). Britain, on the other hand, is scattered and exposed, though certainly this is only because of her "indomitable energy [and] . . . courageous self-dependence," which has allowed her to establish herself around the world: "We are to be reached by a thousand wounds in thousands of outlying extremities. . . . We are the least defended by massy concentration. . . , [China] the most" (180). China, he continues, is "an inorganic mass . . . something to be kicked, but which cannot kick again – having no commerce worth counting, no vast establishments, no maritime industry, no arsenals, no shipbuilding towns . . . in short no vital parts, no organs, no heart, no lungs" ("Opium" 176).

Here the Chinese are reviled for the very vastness of their land; the country is another order of magnitude from that of the smaller being that might want to give it a kick. And while it is De Quincey's aim to insult China by pointing out her lack of maritime industry, he unintentionally reinforces the portrait of China as omnipotent adult to England's small, needy child. The small island kingdom of England is possessed of a flourishing maritime industry precisely because she does not have China's mass and self-sufficiency. The very list of English attainment is a display of its need to be received by and trade with countries such as China. Inadvertently, De Quincey likens England to the child who needs everything from the parent, and China to the parent who seems selfishly to hold everything within herself.

Not only does China have no need of England, but like a cold and disapproving parent, she refuses to recognize the virtues of the smaller land: "They had seen nothing whatever of our national grandeur," De Quincey complains, "nothing of our power; of our enlightened and steadfast constitutional system; of our good faith; of our magnificent and ancient literature; of our colossal charities and provision for every form of human calamity" ("China" 217). And if China sees no good in little England, she also refuses to recognize England's legitimate needs, needs she could easily supply from the vastness of her resources: "What we have to ask from the Chinese was generally so reasonable, and so indispensable to the establishment of our national name upon any footing of equality, that it ought not for a moment to have been tolerated as any subject for debate" ("China" 221).

Like the unresponsive parent, China refuses to use any of her seemingly inexhaustible resources to help the smaller, more vulnerable nation, a nation simply striving, as De Quincey here paints England, to be recognized for her true worth. Instead, China's aim is to "bully" those smaller than herself. And if China is nothing but a bully, it follows that her claims of her own mistreatment are ridiculous. De Quincey derides the assertion, taken seriously by historians and many in England at the time, that the Chinese seizure of opium supplies and detention of Englishmen was the result of an earnest and long-expressed desire to stop the opium that the English, with the help of Chinese smugglers, were illegally pouring into China. To De Quincey, the protest over opium, which triggered British retaliation, was disingenuous. Nobody in China was being hurt by the opium flooding the country, De Quincey writes, as the Chinese were simultaneously too lowly and too depraved to be really harmed. The working class in China, due to the "salutary operation of poverty," could not afford enough opium to create a problem. And the lascivious upper classes were already confirmed opium users: "What a chimerical undertaking to make war upon *their* habits of domestic indulgence!" ("Opium" 168).

Since China has no real claims against the English, since the Chinese are nothing but bullies, it follows for De Quincey that what the Opium War is really about is China's anger over her failure to force the English to degrade themselves through performance of the kowtow to the Chinese emperor. De Quincey was not, of course, the only Englishman to resent the kowtow, a ceremonial gesture which typically included nine bows and three prostrations. It was a ritual traditionally expected of those who came, as the British had come, in supplication to the Chinese. To the Chinese, the kowtow was seen as a gesture of respect, and one routinely practiced among themselves; the emperor himself performed it before his ancestral tablets (Fay 31). To the English, however, it was seen as an act inconsistent with the dignity of free men and one that the British ambassadors refused to perform, and De Quincey, with his keen eye for tyranny and degradation, reveals a near obsession with the kowtow in his writing on China. It could only be the refusal of the English to perform the kowtow, he claims, that drove the Chinese into a frenzy of rage and fueled their protest over British opium: "It was found by the Chinese," De Quincey wrote in the facetious tone that he often took toward them, "that the *ko-tou* would not do. The game was up. Out of this catastrophe, and the wrath which followed it, grew ultimately the opium frenzy of Lin, the mad Commissioner of Canton [who ordered the seizure of British opium]; then the vengeance which followed; next the war, and the miserable defeats of the Chinese. All this followed out of the attempt to enforce the *ko-tou*" ("China" 235). As a weak, sensitive child, the "girlish" De Quincey had no way of avenging himself against those with power over him. In his portrayal of China, however, that is changed. China, first set out as a huge, arrogant, and selfish bully, will also be shown through the magic of vengeful fantasy as a weak and cringing child, and we see that De Quincey himself has now taken the role of bully. The Chinese are derided as having the intellect of children ("China" 201), as being the "silliest" of nations. The emperor is "effeminate," and De Quincey relishes the image of *him* being humiliated, "brought upon his knees and himself subject to 'knock head'" (207). As the Chinese have been turned into bad children, contemptible in their childish weakness as De Quincey once was, their punishment is set out in language redolent of phrases used to describe bad children and their just desserts. Chinese "insolence" must be repressed; the "nuisance" she is causing must be dealt with ("China" 193). She should be "thumped," as this is the only logic the Chinese will understand ("Opium" 174). It is not England's fault if in carrying out these actions China's "girlishness" (190) and "extreme weakness" is revealed (193). Further, no one should think to treat the Chinese gently because of their "childishness" or "girlishness," for the Chinese are "not on that account" the less "knavish or the less dangerous" (190).

In the autobiographical works of "Confessions of an English Opium Eater" and "Suspiria de Profundis," De Quincey replays, as he acknowledges, the "tragedies" of his own "infancy," but he is carefully vague about those who brought about childhood sorrow. He struggles not to "obtrude" his grief upon others, or, when driven to speak, he pretends that these disclosures are incidental to some other primary argument. But in writing about China, as England pumped itself up for the Opium War, De Quincey seems freed from any such constraint; finally he has found a socially approved method of expressing a boundless sense of grief, rage and contempt, even if those who bear the brunt of his wrath have nothing to do with the original injury. In his fabrication of an Asian persona, in his manic attacks upon a people about whom he knows virtually nothing, we see the author obsessively, if unconsciously, reliving the fury of a child at the cold, withholding omnipotence of the parent.

Simultaneously, however, he also wards off his painful sense of his own weakness and victimization by deriding the Chinese – irrationally – for their weakness and unmanliness. This last can be seen, most sadly, in De Quincey's contempt of China as "girlishness," even though we know that in a part of himself De Quincey has wanted nothing more than to find in the world the nurturing tenderness of "girlish" love.

3 ROBERT LOUIS STEVENSON

Imperial Escape

*"I shut my eyes and sail away
And see and hear no more."*
ROBERT LOUIS STEVENSON

Writing out of a childhood that joined an obsession with spiritual and physical weakness to a profound desire for magical escape, Robert Louis Stevenson concocted the literary adventure romance, a genre that would become a chief tool in creating what John MacKenzie calls "an energising myth of Empire" (77). Writers with a more pronounced imperial agenda than Stevenson's, in particular H. Ryder Haggard and Arthur Conan Doyle, took him as a model. With his first romance, *Treasure Island*, Stevenson signaled the shift to what Conan Doyle would call the "modern masculine novel" (Showalter 79), challenging the dominance of the "woman's" novel associated with George Eliot, replacing "inheritance, marriage and death" with danger, adventure and male camaraderie in exotic settings (18).

Stevenson's work had such an impact in part because he drew upon his literary background and upper middle-class connections to press into higher service the vigor and gore of the popular new genre of "penny dreadfuls." Not only could Stevenson lend class to the adventure novel, but he was also psychologically suited for the task of bringing the excitement of the penny dreadfuls into the main stream; his background of morbid religiosity and physical constraint which he countered with dreams of escape seems to have rendered him especially nimble in managing the moral contradictions inherent in both the "manly" adventure story and in many imperial activities. While other authors stumbled over how to link "good" English boys to the acts of violence and treachery sometimes required of one in exotic locales, good and evil co-exist peaceably in Stevenson's early work.

Despite his later success, however, it was not immediately apparent what Stevenson had wrought when *Treasure Island* was published in 1883. Before venturing into romantic adventure, Stevenson had published a series of stories collected as *New Arabian Nights* which portrayed the despairing decadence of young upper class men and were seen as promising by a group of literary friends. At first these friends wrung their hands over *Treasure Island*, fearing that the author – whose relations with his well-to-do father were stormy and whose financial situation was always precarious – was prostituting himself for popular and financial success. Their concern is understandable; the book certainly bore a resemblance to many of those being churned out in the 1880s to attract the newly literate. Such works, which often gloried in the exploits of dashing criminals, were viewed as degraded by the literary establishment, to the point that some feared reading had become an "almost criminal pursuit" (Bristow 32).

Concerns that Stevenson's work might not be "art," however, were put to rest by Henry James in his 1884 essay, "The Art of Fiction," in which James singles out *Treasure Island* as a prime example of literary art, declaring that it succeeds where a work such as Edmond de Goncourt's *Cherie* fails, even though the latter story of the moral development of a child may have been considered by some a more appropriate theme for literature. In claiming *Treasure Island* for art, James declares that tales of "murders," "coincidences" and "buried doubloons" are entirely acceptable themes for respectable fiction, as long as they are contained in a work that reveals "a particular mind, a personal impression of life." In addition to reassuring refined readers that Stevenson's version of "blood and thunder" was respectable, James also absolved them of concern about the probity of such a tale, as he explicitly frees works of fiction from moral constraints. Questions of art, he writes, are questions of "execution; questions of morality are quite another affair." Together, therefore, Stevenson and James launched the adventure novel into the literary main stream, simultaneously freeing it from any "moral" requirement.

By gaining this stamp of literary approval for the adventure novel, Stevenson, though without, it seems, any such intention, helped provide a solution to a problem that was widely perceived in Britain in the 1880s: how to make the newly enfranchised, newly literate working classes understand and identify with imperial interests. For a new theme had been sounded around 1879, as Britain became increasingly aware of threats to overseas dominance from other European countries as well as aspirations for independence by the colonies themselves. It became clear, John MacKenzie writes, that "the idea of Empire" had to be "sold to the great British public" and that there were ways to do the selling. A prime way of "selling" empire was to portray it not as a scheme of financial gain, but as a thrilling adventure. It was understood that the "propaganda appeal of lonely exploration along African rivers, of missionaries converting heathen or, more importantly, of heroic military exploits, was obviously far greater than that of shareholders investing capital in chartered companies" (49). By providing an "artistic" version of the violent thrills found in the "penny dreadful," works of demonstrable appeal both to the young and to the lower classes, and by transporting these thrills to in an exotic foreign clime where great treasure awaited the adventurous and hardy, Stevenson helped create the format for what would become a flood of imperial propaganda, aimed primarily at young readers.

Ironically, *Treasure Island* may serve this need so well precisely because it does not offer justification for imperialism, but rather presents foreign exploits as an adventurous escape from the humdrum of daily life. In the story, the boy Jim, after the death of his anxious and boring innkeeper father, goes off with an adventurous aristocrat and the fabulous pirate, Long John Silver, to search for buried treasure on a distant and uncharted island. On the voyage, the adventurers will have many thrilling experiences while searching for wealth and before returning to resume their places in respectable society. At the end, even the treacherous, murderous Silver is allowed to slip off with a sack of gold. If he will never be quite respectable, he is still expected to "live in comfort" with his loyal wife (*Treasure Island* 151).

The activity associated with empire is thus presented not only as thrilling and ultimately rewarding, but is also undertaken in a sort of moral duty-free zone, smoothly managing the moral contradictions with which imperial Britain must increasingly cope. For, toward the end of the century, some began to question whether empire could be both a high-minded mission to civilize the world, as was so insistently claimed, and simultaneously an opportunity to loot weak countries. Would the deeds done in the name of empire redound to England's everlasting glory, or would they come back to haunt the land, creating, as English Liberal J. A. Hobson suggested, a country whose moral fiber and even physical survival could be destroyed (qtd. in Hobsbawm 83).

In children's publications like *Boys of England*, authors could not avoid an exploration of this duality, but were not always sure how to reconcile these two aspects of imperial England's personality. In "The Story of Jack Rushton," for example, a tale published in *Boys of England* in 1866, there are foreshadowings of *Treasure Island*, as an upright English boy finds himself in the company of a bloody pirate. But, as Joseph Bristow writes, in "Jack Rushton" the "story is rather unsure about how to rationalize [the pirate's] violent history." Both the boy and the pirate "have a part to play in shaping ideal masculinity. But they do not fit easily together. [Young readers] are asked . . . to accept two ostensibly incompatible attitudes – where the law, Christianity, and heartfelt emotions are placed on one side, and merciless, killing, crime and treachery on the other – and see them as belonging to the same world view" (36). The mark of this unresolved conflict is that the boy Jack cannot bring himself to shake hands with the pirate, "because – because," the boy stammers, "your hand is stained with the blood of my poor shipmates" (Haining 306).

By contrast, Stevenson's management of a similar conflict in *Treasure Island* seems effortless, portraying a fruitful and, in the last analysis, non-judgmental co-existence between good and evil. Though Jim has occasion to shudder at Silver's "cruelty, duplicity and power" (*Treasure Island* 50), these characteristics are not without appeal, and Jim is repeatedly and deliciously seduced by Silver's brilliance, charm and buoyant amorality. It is entirely possible, Stevenson's early works suggest, to pursue pleasures and desires that are beyond the bounds of respectable society, to mix with fascinating, if dubious, companions and still be welcomed back into society once the fun is over. In the British schoolroom, increasingly devoted to propagandizing empire, *Treasure Island* became a standard, so that a genre that had earlier been denounced as lowbrow trash came in "a slightly altered form, to be regarded by the next generation as whole-some and patriotic" (Bristow 30).

If the early works of *Treasure Island* and *Kidnapped* seem to allow the conflict between good and evil to dissolve into exotic environments without leaving a trace, Stevenson's later works are very different. These – culminating with his tales of the South Pacific – reveal the tortured underside of this conflict. Like most fantasies of escape from the limita-tions of society and adult responsibilities generally, *Treasure Island* was written by a man still living in conventional circumstances. It will not be until Stevenson is far from England, and until he has to a degree extreme even among adventurous Victorian travelers truly escaped the conven-tions of English society, that his characters will come to grips at last with the incompatible natures of good and evil. Writing from the South Seas in an environment cut loose from traditional constraints, Stevenson will dismay his admirers by undergoing a change. Now he will portray those who leave England for the adventure and treasure of empire not as dash-ingly, forgivably amoral adventurers but as brutal and degraded derelicts.

In the end, it was Stevenson's peculiar mission, not only to give his age what it wanted, but also, finally, to show it what it was. It is possible writes Erik Erikson who was concerned with the interrelationship of the individual and culture, for "a single boy" to "daydream his way into history" so that " a whole nation [may] accept the emotive power of that genius as a hope of fulfillment for its national aspirations and as a warrant for national criminality" (*Young* 109). An examination of Stevenson's experience, as well as the trajectory of his work, will help us better under-stand the "emotive power" that lies beneath the surface of *Treasure Island*, and the psychology of imperial escape.

Stevenson, I will argue, was raised in an environment that placed exces-sive demands upon his emerging psyche, as all three adults in his life appear to have made use of the bright little invalid to achieve, in Erik Erikson's term, "covert emotional relief" for themselves (*Young* 70). Such an environment was an excellent breeding ground for fantasies of strength, freedom and escape, followed by inevitable collapse into a tortured sense of weakness, dependence and depravity.

A life-long invalid, the only child of an invalid mother and a hypochondriac father, Robert Louis Stevenson was brought up in a home where illness was a central obsession and where at least some of his many ailments may have been imagined. With such a background, he was well-suited to speak to a generalized fear of physical impotence and the wish for magical, grandiose triumph over such fear.

Stevenson was confined to bed much of his first nine years with coughs, chills, bronchial infection, gastric infection, and long periods of "fevers, feverish imaginings and sleepless nights" (Calder 29). Unable to attend school regularly, he was often cut off from contact with other children. Throughout his life, until his sudden death of a brain hemorrhage at the age of forty-four, Stevenson was subject to periods of intense illness, often marked by bronchial hemorrhage, and he was frequently thought to be on his deathbed.

Undoubtedly Stevenson was really ill much of the time with what was probably an inherited tendency to bronchial weakness, but as his biographer Jenni Calder notes, "reading of his illnesses one begins to suspect a psychosomatic element" (225); some of his chronic invalidism may have been, at least in part, a result of parental expectations. In adulthood, Stevenson's illnesses included bouts of depression and what Calder terms "something like nervous breakdown," and can often be linked to periods of emotional stress. He was continually ill, for example, in the pleasant Bournemouth house, Skerryvore, purchased for him and his wife by his father, and which seems to have represented his father's bid to reassert control following Stevenson's American marriage. At Skerryvore, Stevenson's friends, such as Henry James, marveled both at the demands the elderly Stevensons put on their son, and also the parents' "blindness" to the effects of these demands(Calder 212). But Stevenson's health improved as if by magic when, only a few years later, he departed on one of many South Seas voyages, even though these were carried out on small boats, in remarkably cramped and rough conditions which would seem to have tried the health of one far more robust.

Stevenson's physical weakness and his fears of spiritual depravity appear to have nourished one another. Illness and long hours in bed prompted a preoccupation with feverish, religious terrors. These fears led to sleepless nights, as anxieties about sin induced sensations of physical pain. If his invalid mother saw her child as constantly threatened by illness, his nurse, Alison Cunningham, who was responsible for virtually all of his care, feared the boy was just as constantly threatened by eternal damnation. "Cummy," in addition to providing careful, twenty-four-hour care, drenched the boy with her own brand of passionate Calvinism, causing him to become, Stevenson would later write, a child given to "high strung religious ecstasies and terrors" (*Memoirs of Himself* 21). If Stevenson's parents' perceptions contributed to his invalidism, it seems certain that Cummy's vision of hellfire created in him anxieties that only Cummy herself could soothe (Calder 34). Writing in California around 1880 at a time when he was extremely ill and seems to be expecting death, Stevenson remembers how he was as a boy given to "hideous nightmares" from which he would awake "screaming in the extreme frenzy of terror" (*Memoirs* 17), and how he would "lie awake to weep for Jesus." He would, he writes, "fear to trust myself to slumber lest I was not accepted and should slip, ere I awoke, into eternal ruin" (21). Such was his anxiety over sin, for example, that he became physically ill after it was hinted to him that a historical story that had been read to him might in fact have been a novel – and thus "worldly." That night, he writes, he began to feel "a pain in my side which frightened me; I began to see Hell pretty clear." The boy decided the pain must have been punishment for having listened to a such a story; the next day he forswore all but religious works. "God help," Stevenson writes ruefully, "the poor little hearts who are thus early plunged among the breakers of the spirit!" (22).

Such an upbringing seems to have contributed powerfully to the moral dualism for which Stevenson is known – both in his early romances and in his classic of duality, *Dr. Jekyll and Mr. Hyde*. His upbringing also seems to have contributed to the obsessive desire for fabulous, if sometimes dangerous, escape. Not only, Stevenson writes in his memoir, did his upbringing make him a "sentimental sniveler" and "morbidly religious," but it also made him secretly fascinated with sin. "I can never again take so much interest in anything, as I took in childhood, in doing for its own sake what I believed to be sinful" (25). And often during the long wakeful nights, he writes, he would invent romances in which "I played the hero. . . . They would always conclude with a heroic and sometimes cruel death. I never left myself till I was dead" (23).

Stevenson's collection of poems, *A Child's Garden of Verses*, is still read to children today as a wry glimpse at generally recognizable childhood fears and fantasies, and undoubtedly this was what the author intended. Looked at more closely, however, the poems, which are dedicated "To Alison Cunningham From Her Boy," reveal the obsessions of the author's early life, and demonstrate the link between a childhood warped by physical and spiritual anxieties, and the impulse to escape through real or image voyages to distant places. Most of the book was written in 1884, when Stevenson, then thirty-four, was confined to his bed in a darkened room with lung and eye ailments. He wrote with his left hand; his right hand was tied to his side, apparently to guard against movement that could prompt further lung hemorrhage (Hennessy 187). Of the poems thus composed, approximately twenty of the sixty five have reference to going to bed, with recurrent mention of sinister forces lurking in the darkness and the longing for day. In "North-west Passage," for example, Stevenson writes of nighttime fears that make the "little heart" of the child go "beating like a drum": "The shadow of the balusters, the shadow of the lamp,/ The shadow of the child that goes to bed/ All the wicked shadows coming tramp, tramp, tramp/ With the black night over-head." Other themes to be found in these poems include thoughts of children existing elsewhere in the world, ideas about how to entertain oneself and be happy ("The world is so full of a number of things/ I'm sure we should all be happy as kings"), and the hope that good behavior will protect one from night terrors. In "A Good Boy," the narrator is happy that he has been well-behaved all day, so that "no ugly dream shall fright my mind, no ugly sight my eyes." Most prominent among the themes of escape, however, is the fantasy of physical flight, often in ships to exotic lands, as the bed of sickness and fear becomes a ship to carry the boy away. In "My Bed is a Boat," he writes, "At night I go on board and say/ Good-night to all my friends on shore;/ I shut my eyes and sail away/ And see and hear no more."

During his earliest years, Stevenson's life appears to have been domi-nated by his mother's invalidism and his nurse's religious fanaticism, both of which kept the boy fearful for his physical and spiritual fate. As an older boy, however, Stevenson was increasingly under the sway of his successful and prominent but depressed and morbidly religious father. Thomas Stevenson was, his son would write, "passionately attached, passionately prejudiced," one who "never accepted the conditions of man's life or his own character" (*Memories* 138). Though Louis remained financially dependent upon his father well into adulthood, he was simul-taneously determined to live a very different sort of life.

Though the elder Stevenson assumed that his son would become another in the family's long line of prominent lighthouse engineers, Louis studied law in Edinburgh. His real interest, however, was writing, developing a bohemian lifestyle, and prowling among Edinburgh's lowlife. An early, real-life version of Mr. Hyde, he appears to be doing everything that a dependent young man could do to reject his father's respectable, religious world view. In an unpublished manuscript written during this time, Stevenson portrays a young man who wants to "slip the leash" and to get "clear away out of our old life and out into the world" (Calder 62). When, during this period, Louis told his parents that he had become an agnostic, his father "hysterically declared that he wished had never . . . had a son, or wished his son dead"; Louis reported to a friend in a letter that his father was praying that God would afflict his son for his sins (Calder 60). So intense was the reaction of both his parents that Stevenson regretted his truthfulness; his parents' response made his expression of his own beliefs too emotionally costly, and appears to echo his childhood in which a separate subjectivity was viewed as a betrayal: "If I had foreseen the real Hell of everything since [the announcement of agnosticism]," he wrote in a letter, "I think I should have lied . . . they are both ill, both silent" (Calder 60).

Indeed, the troubled relationship between a dominant father figure and a rebellious but finally weak son is the primary theme of Stevenson's first published short stories, written at a time when Stevenson was still being supported by his father. The stories first published in 1878 and collected in 1882 as *New Arabian Nights*, revolve around young men who try but finally fail to escape the hold of established, wealthy, often hypocritical older men. The younger, more idealistic men in the stories simply can not stand up to these powerful and supremely confident elders, and even the moral positions taken by the younger men erode in the face of this overwhelming force. In "A Lodging for the Night," for example, a nihilistic, upper-class young man slums among criminals. On a freezing night, having lost all his money and with no place to go, he takes food, drink and shelter from a wealthy older man. The price for this "lodging," however, is to be subjected to the older man's unbearably smug self-righteousness. In "The Sire de Maletroit's Door," an old man kidnaps a young knight and gives him the choice of either marrying his niece or dying at dawn. The courageous and noble young man initially refuses, but by morning the two young people have fallen in love and the old man's machinations have succeeded. In none of the stories do the younger men succeed in asserting themselves against their more confident and powerful elders.

Stevenson's first real-life bid for escape from his father's influence and support did not come until 1879 when he left Scotland unannounced and traveled to California to join Fanny Osbourne, an American woman ten years older than himself whom he had met in France. Osbourne had left a philandering husband in a Western mining town to come to Europe with her two children to study art. The older Stevensons' horror at this move on the part of their thirty-year-old son seems to have gone well beyond what might be considered normal for parents dismayed at a child's choices. The Stevensons seemed to feel that Louis's departure for America had literally destroyed them; they claimed to be "half-murdered," and even talked of leaving Scotland and moving to a place where they were not known to escape the shame of their son's conduct. In a letter, Thomas wrote that he saw "nothing but destruction [for Louis] as well as to all of us" (Calder 134).

Thomas Stevenson's responses to his son's bid to pursue his own inclinations are so extreme that they suggest his inability to see his son as the center of his own life even as an adult, and correspondingly his own profound dependence upon seeing his son as a reflection of himself. Interestingly, something very similar to the outrage and rejection expressed by Stevenson's conventional parents is also displayed by some of his literary friends who repeatedly express that Louis has no right to "abandon" them and England, and who seek to repress the writing that he does in America.

W. R. D. Fairbairn believed that adults pattern their later relationships on earlier ones, and unconsciously accept from others the types of emotional interaction they have had with their early caregivers (Mitchell 121). Alice Miller also posits that the adult "unconsciously reenacts" his early relationships with those he encounters later as a way of "indirectly rediscovering" the truth of his experience (19). Reading his mail in California, Stevenson found that neither his friends nor his parents were able to support him in his American adventure.

While Charles Baxter supported Louis without criticism, William Henley and Sidney Colvin wrote to Louis and each other in a tone that has a distinctly parental ring: "It is absolutely necessary," Henley wrote Colvin, "that he should be brought to see that England and a quiet life are what he wants and must have if he means to make – I won't say a reputation – but money by literature" (qtd. in Calder 139). Not only did Henley disapprove of Louis's actions, he also could not grant that they might be based on legitimate feeling: "He has gone too far to retract," Henley wrote Colven, "He has acted & gushed and excited himself too nearly into the heroic spirit to be asked to forbear his point" (Calder 140).

Further, even though two of Stevenson's earlier books were based upon his travels, both parents and friends expressed disapproval not only of Stevenson himself, but also of the work inspired by the American trip. "You may expect that Louis will resent our criticism of his latest three works," Henley wrote Colvin, "But I think it right he should get them. . . . Monterey will never produce anything worth a damn" (Hennessy 156). Meanwhile his father went so far as to suppress publication of *An Amateur Emigrant*, which portrays in realistic terms his son's journey from Scotland to California in the company of humble, immigrant travelers. Jonathan Rabin, writing an introduction to the posthumously published work in 1984 finds it to be the "best account ever written" of the journey from Europe to America, one which has the "reasonance and simplicity of myth." Stevenson's father, however, declared the book to be the worst thing Stevenson had ever done and "altogether unworthy." Henley labeled the work "feeble, stale and pretentious" (Hennessy 141).[1]

The "avalanche" of disapproval Stevenson had gotten from home added to Stevenson's miseries in California where he had no money, and where he and Fanny were both ill. When Edmund Gosse wrote Stevenson a friendly letter, Louis responded with gratitude for the "act of friendship" which came in the midst of "horrid feuds with threatening letters" and telegrams. "I give you my word of honour, Gosse, I am trying to behave well, and in some sort, which is as much as one can say, succeeding" (Calder 140).

Stevenson's parents and to some extent his friends would ultimately be reconciled with both him and his wife. But their outraged responses to Stevenson's California adventure is telling. Both had made much of Stevenson's brilliance and charm, but in his first real bid for independence both seem to betray the expectation that the precocious creature would stay within their control. Though Stevenson's friends had applauded his rejection of Scottish piety to embrace artistic bohemianism, they appeared to be as shocked as his parents by Stevenson's bid to strike out on his own. "Louis was *their* charge," Calder writes of Stevenson's friends. "He had no business to be gallivanting off independently, beyond their care or help." They had "cultivated his talent and career, and here he was taking impossible risks" (140).

The child of narcissistic parents is taught that "strivings toward autonomy" will be experienced by the parents as an "attack," that assertion of a separate self can have terrible consequences, psychically destroying or enraging the parent, which can result in the child's abandonment (Miller 33). Stevenson, at least in the early years of his life and career, can be seen to fluctuate between two states – the desire for magical escape, and the sense that the bid for freedom will result in physical or spiritual death, perhaps both. Like the little boy who read the thrilling history, then spent the night in physical pain and in fear that his worldliness would be punished by hellfire, the young adult must pay for his escape with physical and psychic suffering. On his voyage to California to reach Fanny Osbourne, he seemed to break free of all that had imprisoned him in Britain. He had rejected Cummy's Calvinism, his father's profession and even, for a time, put himself in a position where he had to function without his father's money. In addition, he had, temporarily at least, abandoned his literary British friends, who initially appeared to represent a break from parental control, but soon begin to replicate it. This bid to escape, however, was drenched in physical and psychic pain. Throughout the trip, he was extremely ill, frightening others with his skeletal appearance. In the memoir written during this time, he appears to think himself near death, and is threatened with a serious loss of identity. As is consistent with narcissistic injury as described by Heinz Kohut he appears to be unable to integrate the part of himself that is controlled and fearful, with the part that imagines soaring triumph. Traveling by immigrant train through Ohio, he seemed to feel himself disappearing, and writes to a friend, "There seems nothing left of me. I died a while ago and know not who it is that is traveling" (qtd. in Hennessy 146). In the memoir written in California he portrays himself as alone, ill and penniless, with missives of resentment and disapproval his only connection to family and friends in England. Here too he seems to perceive himself as one no longer alive, who can only wait to be annihilated as a punishment for his bid to assert a separate self: "I seem to be cured of all my adventurous whims and even human curiosity," he writes, "and am content to sit here by the fire and await the course of fortune . . . I know myself no longer" (13).

But Stevenson's mood changed after he succeeded in marrying the unconventional Fanny, who, already a mother and soon to be a grandmother, would nurse and protect him throughout a life lived in truly outlandish circumstances. Fanny, unlike Stevenson's British friends and family, appears to have been able to see and accept both sides of the man at once, his dependent, fearful, invalid self, and the self that constantly sought to soar beyond the bonds of convention. As a result, Fanny spent most of her married life simultaneously nursing Louis in almost constant illness, and also arranging and managing one fantastic voyage after another.[2]

Marriage to Fanny and life with her young son Lloyd appear to have opened a door for Stevenson, as *Treasure Island*, written a year after his marriage, is a work markedly different from his previous fiction. The theme of Stevenson's earlier tales was of a rebellious but weak younger man who tries but fails to prevail in a confrontation with a well-established older man of conventional if somewhat hypocritical morality. Now that story is all but turned on its head. The young hero of *Treasure Island*, Jim, does not need to rebel against powerful men, as these men themselves – once Jim's tedious inn-keeper father conveniently dies – are engaged in an unconventional and, at times, morally dubious adventure. Not only has Jim played a key role from the beginning by finding a pirate's map thus making him valuable to the men who arrange the voyage, but he appears to be a favorite of the ship's cook, later revealed to be the cunning pirate Long John Silver who embodies all of the free-wheeling, amoral adventurousness a boy could wish.

Partnered with Silver, Stevenson's young hero can be both "good" and free at once. As a decent young boy, Jim is properly shocked when he learns that the cook is really a dangerous pirate who plans to take over the expedition, and shudders when Silver's blood-thirsty intentions are revealed (50). Silver is no sanitized villain; we hear the screams of the honest seaman he murders, and Jim eyes him warily as if he is "a snake about to spring" (61). But Stevenson presents Silver's free-wheeling life as so appealing that the good boy, Jim, simply has no choice but to be ravished. Silver "made himself the most interesting companion, telling me about the different ships we passed . . . or repeating a nautical phase till I had learned it perfectly. I began to see that here was one of the best possible shipmates" (36).

Though Silver is a vicious pirate, he is no "common man," has had schooling, can "speak like a book when so minded." He is neat and clean, wins the respect of everyone on board, and, along with these homely virtues, he is fearless. "A lion's nothing alongside of Long John," notes an admiring companion (42). In this way too he is the sort of villain a respectable boy can admire.

Once they reach the island and Silver's intentions are clear, Jim tries to do the proper thing and ally himself with the more upright members of the expedition who are embattled with Silver and the pirates. Through a misunderstanding, however, the respectable men turn against Jim. This solves Jim's moral dilemma nicely, as now he has no choice but to ally with Silver, and to, in a sense, *become* Silver. "I've always liked you," Silver tells Jim, "I have, for a lad of spirit and the picter of my own self when I was young and handsome. I always wanted you to jine and take your share and die a gentleman, and now, my cock, you've got to" (120).

Here we see Stevenson finally managing to envision a successful escape from the controlling physical and moral environment of his childhood. In exotic foreign environments, it seems, acts of rebellion need not be punished with fears of physical and psychic annihilation. Jim is never punished for enjoying his temporary alliance with the thrilling Silver, nor is Silver himself punished for his murderous deeds. In the end, he goes on his way, the richer for his adventure. As Robert Fraser notes approvingly, the book allows readers to "forget the nagging conflict between Good and Evil" and regress to a "toy-theatre world" (26).

Surely, in Stevenson's personal case, it is a beginning step along the road to psychic health to be able imagine successful – if temporary – integration between the "good" aspect of the self with the part that yearns for release from the constraints of others. Still, it must also be noted that this book which will become a schoolroom standard does not present a maturely integrated vision of the struggle between grandiose and amoral infantile desires for escape, on one hand, and on the other, the compromises one must embrace to live in a world where one is not the omnipotent center of life.

Though Stevenson was, after *Treasure Island*, a married man and the well-known author of a successful novel, he was once again being supported by his father, who had accepted the marriage once it was accomplished and purchased a home for the newlyweds, Skerryvore in Bournmouth. Here Stevenson found himself once again living under the thumb of his pious and respectable father. The elder Stevensons visited constantly, and seemed intent on reasserting their claim to their son. Louis's literary friends were also nearby and seem to have been intent upon renewing their claims as well. Some feuded with Fanny, protesting when she tried to cut short late-night partying in the cause of protecting her husband's health. Stevenson's physical condition deteriorated during this period, and would continue to do so until the Stevensons began their lives as South Seas nomads when his health improved "amazingly" (Calder 246). At Skerryvore, however, ill and depressed, subject to the attentions of controlling family and friends, the idea of uniting the parts of the self in a magical setting seems to have been temporarily lost, and to be replaced by the fantasy of a hero who resists all constraints, but who is doomed for his rebellion to suffer "cruel death."

In *Dr. Jekyll and Mr. Hyde*, written in bed in Bournemouth between lung hemorrhages, Stevenson speaks to Victorian duality in a different way than in *Treasure Island*. In a sense, *Dr. Jekyll and Mr. Hyde* pays the bill left due by *Treasure Island*. If *Treasure Island* allows a "good" and well-bred boy to nevertheless enjoy the pleasures of unconventionality and amorality without penalty or tarnish, here there is no viable co-existence between the upright, admirable and dour Jekyll and the evil, deformed and orgiastic Hyde, even though they are one; ultimately they must destroy one another.

There is much in this tale that is reminiscent not only of Stevenson's childhood of invalidism and obsession with sin, but also of the intense and ongoing relationship with his controlling, sternly Calvinist father. The child who is required to respond to the wishes of others rather than to his own emerging needs, has difficulty developing a sense of subjectivity, Winnicott writes, and of a separate and inviolable self. In this work there is a horror both that what one may glimpse of one's separate self is hideously deformed and evil, and also that this self, though glimpsed, can never really live, can never escape the internalized parental demands.

There are many indications that Hyde stands as evil child, obsessed by forbidden pleasures, in relation to Jekyll's respectable, repressed father figure. In his "statement" at the end of the story, Dr. Jekyll in effect identifies the two personas who inhabit his body as good father and bad son: "Jekyll had more than a father's interest" in Hyde's doings, he writes, while Hyde "had more than a son's indifference" (114). Jekyll, an "elderly" doctor, "surrounded by friends and cherishing honest hopes," is contrasted to Hyde, whose pleasures are youthful; he enjoys "liberty . . . comparative youth, [a] light step, leaping impulses and secret pleasures" (115). Not only does Hyde appear to be younger than Jekyll, but though they share the same body, he is also smaller and somehow deformed; he swims in Dr. Jekyll's large clothing like a child who has put on grown-up attire. As fathers sometimes bail their sons out of financial trouble, Jekyll signs the checks to make restoration for Hyde's evil deeds. Hyde will be the beneficiary of Jekyll's will. And while Jekyll reads improving books by the safe and comfortable fireside, Hyde plays childish "ape-like" tricks that mock Jekyll's pious respectability. Some of these tricks, Jekyll writes, are "scrawling in my own hand blasphemies on the pages of my books, burning the letters and destroying the portrait of my father" (123). When Hyde kills, it is with the unreasonable fury with which "a sick child may break a plaything" (116).

Further, much of Hyde's anger in the story, appears to be the anger of a desperate younger man enraged by the self-satisfied virtue of older, respectable figures. A witness sees Hyde encounter an old man who seems to embody an "innocent and old world kindness" and a "well founded self-content." The old man with a polite manner appears to be asking Hyde directions, reports a witness, when the younger man flies into a rage and "with ape-like fury" strikes and tramples his victim until his "bones were audibly shattered and the body jumped on the roadway" (60). Later we are told of the "glee" that Hyde felt at killing the fine old man, and the sensation that in committing this brutal act his "love of life was screwed to the topmost peg" (116). We see here an enraged reprise of Stevenson's *New Arabian Nights* stories. The violence and outright criminality are new, but the attempts of a younger man to free himself from dependency on a pious, self-satisfied father figure are familiar.

Though Hyde is presented as being as unrepentantly evil as possible, committing deeds that are too horrible to be mentioned or possibly even imagined, these evil acts appear to flow from a remarkably unobjectionable source. Again we are prompted to read Hyde as, at bottom, a child, and his rage as the predictable result of repeatedly thwarting a child's natural instincts. For the aspect of Jekyll, that must be split off into Hyde, appears to be nothing worse than a "gaiety of disposition." Jekyll understands that for others, gaiety could lead to happiness, but for him such light-heartedness cannot be reconciled with "an imperious desire to carry my head high, and wear a more than commonly grave countenance" (103) and so it had to be repressed. In the world of Jekyll and Hyde it is impossible that rectitude and propriety could be combined with a sense of freedom and fun. Rather, to give in to one's desires for escape from stern propriety leads to corruption and death, even though the desire for freedom is so intense, that it simply must out, no matter the consequences.[3]

It was not until 1887, the year after *Dr. Jekyll and Mr.Hyde* was published, that Stevenson would make his final escape from England, going with Fanny, Lloyd and his widowed mother, Margaret Stevenson, first to Saranac Lake, New York, then to San Francisco. There with the financial backing of Sam McClure, who engaged Stevenson to write weekly articles for *World* magazine, the family entourage chartered a yacht to sail to the South Seas. By now his domineering father was dead and Stevenson was famous and financially self-sufficient. He was far from the friends who demanded, complained and accused, and who were, McClure reported "very much annoyed by the attention [Stevenson] had received in America" (Hennessy 257). And now in the cramped, damp quarters of a small yacht, his health was "amazingly" improved, and he began to send back an entirely different sort of writing than anything to have come before.

It appears to have been Stevenson's fate to embody tortured Victorian duality – respectable probity versus the desire for magical escape – to such an extreme degree that he was forced to literally and permanently flee its site. Ironically, in doing so, he appears to have come face to face with the fact that, no matter where one goes, one can not really return to a state of infantile amorality without disastrous consequence. Understanding this at last, Stevenson loses his ability to serve as the voice of longing for escape from adult proprieties. If *Treasure Island* presents a tropical island as a setting where one could undertake piratical escapades without fear of punishment, Stevenson's actual experience in the South Seas destroys this fantasy. The South Seas, as recorded by Stevenson, is not a place where one can safely forget the "nagging conflict" between good and evil, but rather a place where the costs of self-indulgent amorality are only too apparent.

Against the intense disapproval of some of his friends – whose investment in the fantasy of escape appears to be matched only by their fury at one who actually throws off traditional constraints – Stevenson begins to act as if the South Seas is a real place where actions have consequences, devoting himself to researching and writing about the role of Europeans and the Americans in the Pacific and the damage done to indigenous lives and culture. Though his friends predicted that such themes would seriously damage his image as writer of romances, Stevenson began to produce a series of articles denouncing what he considered to be shameful imperial activities (Calder 309). Even Fanny feared that Louis's work was becoming too "stodgy," but he persisted in a program of serious study of native language, culture, religion and politics with the aim of educating Europeans to the real nature of the South Pacific.

It must be acknowledged that Stevenson's sojourn in the South Pacific replicated, in many ways, that of the imperialists he condemns. He arrived with a sense of entitlement, never seeming to question whether he was wanted or whether he was, at bottom, only another white who felt entitled to use of the islands for his own purposes. And he was comfortable taking on the role of "chief and father," not only to those who lived and worked in the large house he eventually built – the Samoans who worked for him asked his permission to marry (Calder 311) – but also to the community generally, seeing himself as the "moral and political centre of the island's life" (297).

It may also be claimed that Stevenson, at least to some extent, used the natives as a screen upon which to project his own transgressive desires, choosing locations to visit where he believed the population to be the "most beastly." Further, in the journalistic writing published posthumously as *In the South Seas*, we may detect that Stevenson makes

Robert Louis Stevenson in bed in Villa Vailima. Credited by Arthur Conan Doyle with creating the "modern masculine novel" and frequently seen as the father of the literary adventure romance genre, Stevenson was also a life-long invalid who did much of his writing sitting up in bed. Here he plays a flageolet in bed in his Samoan villa.

psychological use of the natives in another way, seeing them, in their physical and cultural decline, as representing one aspect of himself, oppressed and ill, waiting fatalistically for death. In this, Stevenson resembles the writer Karen Blixen, who, in *Out of Africa,* consciously portrays herself as a beloved feudal lord to the Africans she has displaced. She both admires the African's sense of natural entitlement to be themselves, and also compares their disenfranchisement to her own psychic losses.

But unlike Blixen's work, Stevenson's writings on the South Pacific are marked by an unrelenting effort to see things as they are; the man who theorized romance for a generation now takes pride that he has written the first non-romance of the South Seas: "It is the first realistic South Sea story," he wrote of "The Beach of Falesá." "Everybody else who has tried . . . got carried away by the romance, and ended in a kind of sugar candy sham epic . . . Now I have got the smell and look of the thing a good deal. You will know more about the South Seas after you have read my little tale than if you read a library" (qtd. in Jolly xxvii).

Stevenson's "realism" results in brutal honesty about the destructive impact of the incursion of whites. Stevenson, for example, mocks the Europeans' claim that the islanders have demonstrated their moral inferiority by their failure to adopt European beliefs. The islander, he writes, "had been forced at the point of the bayonet to destroy the sacred places of his own piety; when he had recoiled from the task, he had been jeered at for a superstitious fool. And now it is supposed he will respect our European superstitions by second nature" (*South Seas* 96). In his letters he could hardly be more frank. Left to themselves, he believed, the Samoans were "a healthy happy people;" the Europeans who have supposedly come to improve their lives are a "hollow fraud," engaged in a "dance of folly and injustice and unconscious rapacity" (qtd. in Jolly xiii).

And though Stevenson is willing to become a "chief," he does not, as does Blixen, suppose that the natives admire him and other whites as godlike figures. Rather he understands that the natives on some level regard Europeans with justifiable horror: "I believe all natives regard white blood as a kind of talisman against the powers of hell. In no other way can they explain the unpunished recklessness of Europeans" (*South Seas* 139).

If the Europeans in *In the South Seas* are not good, neither are they strong and capable. There is no hint here of the White Man's Burden, of the "best" of breed sent out to "fill the mouth of Famine/ And bid the sickness cease" (Kipling 52). Rather, the whites who find their way to the South Pacific are often "broken" men, "living on the bounty of the natives" (*South Seas* 10). Previously the laureate of romantic escape, Stevenson now, in both fiction and non-fiction, portrays whites who have voyaged to the South Pacific not as charming pirates, fascinating, brave, and ultimately successful in their bold deeds, but rather, in a thesis that will be argued by Albert Memmi many years later, as pathetic losers who have come out to the colonies because they are failures at home.

In the novel *Ebb Tide,* for example, three degenerate beachcombers cannot manage to successfully steal a ship, as they are too preoccupied with drinking up its cargo of champagne. The three are forced to land on an uncharted island where most of the population has succumbed to small pox. The island is ruled by an Englishman, Attwater, a character who could have served as a precursor to Kurtz, the trader who sets himself up as a god to his African subjects in Joseph Conrad's 1902 novella, *Heart of Darkness.* Attwater is arrogant, sadistic, and more than a little mad in his simultaneous megalomania and weepy religiosity. Self-exiled, he has spent ten years wringing a fortune in pearls from the island's inhabitants so he can return to England a rich man to marry his beloved. When the three drifters wash up on his shore, he is at pains to show his contempt for the ill-bred Cockney, Huish, and to court Herrick, who, despite his present degeneracy was once a "university man." Upon hearing Attwater describe how, before he killed a native worker, he toyed with the man, who "whimpered like a dog," his "eyes bulging," Herrick runs away. Sickened by these horrors, he tries to kill himself. But he doesn't have the nerve, and can do nothing but crawl back to the protection of Attwater, whom he despises. "I have nothing left to believe in," Herrick says, "except my living horror of myself" (228).

Here again, is the theme of "escape," but in this story the more the men try to escape the difficult dilemmas, obligations and sacrifices of maturity, the more wretched they become so that death seems preferable. In this vision there is no fabulous Silver, charming, interesting, full of life and vigor, ultimately free. There is only Attwater, cold, snobbish, hypocritical, sadistic, inescapable, presiding over an island of death. In the end, *Ebb Tide* is a dark vision of the doomed attempt to use conquered, exotic lands as a site of return to a state of infantile amorality and irresponsibility. Here, to flee civilization's rules and adults' moral responsibilities is to descend into the most wretched degeneracy.

But other tales, such as "The Beach of Falesá," and "The Bottle Imp," written at around the same time and collected in *Island Nights Entertainments,* signal something new. For the first time in Stevenson's fiction we see something approaching a mature acceptance both of one's own imperfections and also of the responsibilities one owes to others. Stevenson's early stories are ultimately static, all-male scenarios; though there are dysfunctional male couples made up of powerful father figures and helplessly discontented sons, the protagonists are, as Barry Menikoff has observed of Francis Villon in "A Lodging for the Night," "essentially alone in the world and forced to live with that condition" (12). Against this background, the connections in the South Seas stories come as a surprise. Here are men who have relationships with women, and in "The Beach of Falesá," even children, and who, though they are far from conventionally proper, are, for the first time, concerned for the happiness and well-being of others than themselves.

In these stories, the South Seas is still a place of awful degeneracy, and Stevenson bitterly mocks the Europeans who have come to exploit the place as well as the ludicrous justifications with which some bother to paper over their actions. In "The Beach of Falesá," which also anticipates Conrad's *Heart of Darkness*, a young man arrives on a remote island to run a trading station after the deaths and desertion of previous managers. Here he finds two rivals in the project of extracting wealth from the natives. The first is a former ship's captain whose life in the exotic South Seas has left him as nearly decomposed as a living man can be. He is seen "squatting on the floor native fashion, fat and pale, naked to the waist, grey as a badger, and his eyes set with drink." His body is covered with flies, one of which crawls unhindered in his eye (*Short Stories* 576). The decomposition experienced by the other rival, Case, is more moral than physical; a master in the art of religious hypocrisy, he pretends that he has supernatural powers so that he can frighten the natives into doing his will.

Upon arrival, the narrator, Wiltshire, appears to be heading down the same road as his fellow traders, participating in a cynical wedding ceremony that makes a travesty of traditional European vows. Since missionaries have decreed that marriages be documented, the traders have devised a mockery of a wedding license which gives the groom the right to send his bride "to hell when he pleases" (580).

Wiltshire, whose original ambition is simply to get enough money to go home and open a public house, presents himself to the natives with the ludicrous pomposity of a true loser: "You tell them who I am. I'm a white man, and a British subject, and no end of a big chief at home; and I've come here to do them good and bring them civilization" (594). In expressing his satisfaction at getting the native Kanakas to "knuckle under" to self-defeating propositions, he is given a speech that is scathing in its portrayal of an untroubled if irrational sense of white superiority and entitlement: "They haven't any real government or any real law, that's what you've got to knock into their heads; and even if they had, it would be a good joke if it was to apply to a white man. It would be a strange thing if we came all this way and couldn't do what we pleased" (595).

At first it seems that the narrator, like Jim in *Treasure Island*, will easily fit into the world of the other traders, that he will, like other of Stevenson's young protagonists, ultimately have no recourse but to admire and succumb to the amoral power of a man like Case. But here Stevenson introduces a new option, partnership with a loving woman, in this case Wiltshire's native wife Uma. Though he has married her in the utmost cynicism, and though her cooking is terrible and her logic maddening, she turns out to be loving, devoted and courageous. At the story's climax, she comes, despite near paralyzing terror, to a forest she believes to be haunted to warn her husband of Case's plot to murder him. *Treasure Island* was praised for creating a world where one could avoid the "nagging conflict between Good and Evil." Here, however, Stevenson's protagonist jumps squarely into this conflict on the side of good, destroying the vile Case in the name of those he has harmed: "'Do you feel the point of that? That's for Underhill! And here's for Adams! And now here's for Uma, and that's going to knock your blooming soul right out of you'" (644).

Finally, greed, cruelty, and amoral opportunism have lost their charm for Stevenson's protagonists, and his characters have lost their ability to slip the knot of consequence. Stevenson, it appears, cannot help but to see and finally to despise what such attitudes have wrought for the people of the South Pacific. In *Dr. Jekyll and Mr. Hyde* Stevenson indulged in violence, but it was the violence of evil destroying innocence, the vision, I believe, of a young man who still romanticized the exotic magic of sin. Here is the reverse as Wiltshire ferociously and vengefully destroys a man who represents human degradation. And in the visceral language, in the *pleasure* Wiltshire takes in destroying this wretched man who has preyed on so many innocent people, I think we read that Wiltshire – like Stevenson – has undergone a conversion that we are meant to take seriously. Once thoughtlessly seduced by the vision of amoral pleasure and plunder, he now hates it; Wiltshire reports that he "give[s] [Case] the knife again a half a dozen times up to the handle. I believe he was dead already, but it did him no harm and did me good" (645). Seeing the dead Case, Wiltshire feels like singing and whistling. "Talk about meat and drink! Seeing him lying there dead like a herring filled me full" (646). This, I think, is a righteous murder.

Further, I believe Stevenson is making another point with this story: there may come a time when one finally manages to give up childish fantasies and embrace an imperfect adult reality. This story with its hatred of those who would prey on others, and its acceptance of an imperfect adult reality is a long way from the first stories of nihilistic and superior young men, from the amoral adventures of the romances, and from the unspeakable desires and tortured duality of *Jekyll and Hyde*. Here, as the story closes, the narrator realizes he'll never return to England with a fortune to open his public house. He will stay with his wife, who, though no exotic siren, is a pretty good pal. He'll stay with his children, even though they are only girls and half castes at that. Wiltshire is still no saint; he's still a product of a European world view and "there's nobody thinks less of half casts than I do." But it's not a perfect world and he'll stay because "they're mine and they're about all I've got" (649).

Erik Erikson has written, "now and again . . . an individual is called upon . . . to lift his individual patienthood to the level of a universal one and to try to solve for all what he could not solve for himself alone" (*Young* 67). It appears to have been Stevenson's role to attempt to "solve" – in art and life – the Victorian desire for magical escape, both from the griefs and weaknesses of childhood, and from the compromises and responsibilities of adulthood. But the solution he ultimately provided was not one that pleased his admirers. In actually making his escape to the most exotic locale he could image, he described the limits of grandiose fantasy. The result was a palpable sense of betrayal on the part of Stevenson's admirers who needed Stevenson to continue to play the role of "boy traveler" (Swinnerton 61).

After the author's death, his friend W. E. Henley decried the man Stevenson had become; he was "not my old, riotous, intrepid, scornful Stevenson at all." For Henley, the "real" Stevenson was the "unmarried and irresponsible" young man he had known in Edinburgh (Calder 321). Oscar Wilde perhaps expressed best the sense of the loss that many felt as Stevenson sent reports back from a world that had previously existed only in fantasy: "I see that romantic surroundings are the worst surroundings possible for a romantic writer. In Gower Street Stevenson could have written a new *Trois Mousquetaires*. In Samoa, he wrote letters to the *Times* about Germans" (qtd. in Jolly xxix). Even more telling, perhaps, is the fact that Stevenson's South Seas tales were simply ignored when, after Stevenson's death, critics assessed his contribution. "It was as if," Jolly writes, "this body of work simply did not exist" (xxx).

4 CONAN DOYLE

The Curse of Empire

"It was an era of profound identity crisis and transformation for a bour-geoisie whose traditional moral foundation crumbled under the very pressure of its own accumulations of wealth and comfort."

ERIC HOBSBAWM

Voluminous as the public discussion of British imperialism was in books, children's magazines, sermons and speeches, it generally stuck to an elab-oration of glowing self-image and lofty ideals, and failed to mention the material advantages which empire could bestow. This was the case even though the ease with which technologically advanced countries could defeat and exploit traditional societies was both relatively new and stun-ning in its implications. Suddenly, poorer countries "were all equally at the mercy of ships that came from abroad bringing cargoes of goods, armed men and ideas against which they were powerless" (Hobsbawm 20). The British public, therefore, was required to live with a significant degree of duality in regard to imperial activities. Empire was insistently viewed as a high-minded mission to civilize the world, even though everyone knew it was simultaneously an opportunity to loot poor countries. Toward the end of the century, the "questionable morality" of empire had to be both "discreetly suppressed" and at times "deeply repressed" (Druce 191). Despite this repression, the subject continually surfaced in popular literature, where wealth brought back from abroad was a theme upon which many works turned. During the later years of empire, it became the task of popular literature to manage a repressed but corrosive guilt over imperial "loot," a constant battle against a feared curse of empire.

One writer who negotiated between the poles of imperial grandiosity and imperial guilt was Arthur Conan Doyle, whose phenomenally popular detective and modern-day knight, Sherlock Holmes, embodies a wish for magical superiority. Like the child's fantasized omniscient parent, Holmes easily solves the seemingly unsolvable. At the same time, however, we can detect in these stories the guilty, fearful underside of grandiosity, as the majority of cases Holmes must solve are caused not by a common crime but by a combination of foreign contamination and the guilt engendered by dubious imperial deeds.

The Sherlock Holmes stories, however, are not overtly about empire; rather empire is a background taint, constantly seeping into British life. It appears that this sense of imperial blowback is unconscious, since when consciously writing about empire, Conan Doyle sticks to a formula that stridently contrasts British perfection with the inferiority of other nations and races. In his historical novel, *The White Company*, for example, the English are portrayed as morally superior to the French and Spanish they encounter. The English are jocular when killing a black man, a character brought in solely for this purpose it seems; the narrator admits that a black man is "a thing rarely met" in 14th century England. But they grow cold and stern when the Continentals seem to compare the English class system to their own, or to suggest that an Englishman might cheat on his wife (199–200).

Further, the English are shown to be destined for world dominance, a fact that is visible to a 14th Century spiritualist who cries: "My God what is this shown to me? Whence come they, these peoples, these lordly nations, these mighty countries which rise up before me. . . . The world is given to them, and it resounds with the clang of hammers and the ringing of church bells. They call them many names, and they rule them this way or that, but they are all English" (256).

But it was not such historical works that turned Conan Doyle's name into a household word in a matter of months. Rather it was the imitative, hastily written and shoddily researched detective stories that became a national craze. "Each issue of the *Strand Magazine* was ardently awaited at news stands," Booth writes, where "queues formed on publication day. Arthur Conan Doyle was soon a household name. . . . In a matter of months Sherlock Holmes was as well known as Queen Victoria and better known than many of the leading political figures of the time" (145).

Conan Doyle, who had hoped to become known as a writer of historical fiction like his idol Sir Walter Scott, was not happy with his success. Though he could command unheard of fees for the detective stories, he resented that his fame was based on work in a form he considered inferior. As the success of the stories became apparent, he was "all nerves, unable to sleep," and stricken with influenza so that he "almost died at exactly the moment he became nationally famous" (Higham 96). He soon came to hate the stories he had created, and in 1892 caused a national uproar by trying to kill the detective off in "The Final Problem" where Holmes plunges over a waterfall to his death. The result was a public outcry as more than 20,000 people canceled their subscriptions to the

Strand Magazine. "Abusive mail arrived at the editorial offices by the sackload whilst hundreds more letters were sent directly to Conan Doyle beseeching him to reverse Holmes's death." There were dozens of news stories and obituaries, and "people wore black armbands in public mourning" (Booth 190). Eventually Conan Doyle acquiesced in bringing Holmes back with a play in 1897, and then accepted an offer to bring out six more stories for fees that "were the highest ever paid to an author up to that time." Conan Doyle's attitude toward the new stories was one of "cynicism." Still, the first story, "The Adventure of the Empty House," was a "blockbuster" when it appeared, and fans crowded and elbowed to get their copies (Booth 248).

These stories, I suggest, were so phenomenally popular in part because they addressed a need to manage the ongoing struggle between two parts of the English psyche, a grandiose image of British powers on one hand; on the other, the sense of a growing vulnerability. The Sherlock Holmes stories show that the problems of empire have found their way into the heart of British life. As Stephen Knight has shown, the stories deal with threats that, generally speaking, "come from within the family and the class, not from enemy criminals" in the form of a "selfish greed which cuts across normal family responsibility" (370). I would add that what makes such "greed" particularly destructive in many of the stories are the opportunities for exploitation that exist abroad, making empire an agent of one's own worst self.

If it is this mixture of guilt, threatened breakdown, and near-magical solutions that accounted for the appeal of the detective stories, the same mixture may also explain Conan Doyle's hatred of them. For in their central dilemmas and solutions they are reflections of a past the author tried all of his life to suppress, a childhood of shame, poverty and mental instability which was escaped through descent into fantasies of greatness or magical otherworldliness.

Like the many disinherited or impoverished black sheep in the Sherlock Holmes stories, Conan Doyle's father, Charles Doyle, was the unstable youngest son of a prominent family. Like them, he dreamed of reversing his fortunes in Australia, but in his case the dream was never realized. Rather, he married the daughter of his landlady with whom he would have nine children, Arthur being the third child and first son. Mary and Charles Doyle lived in genteel poverty, moving from one location to another in Edinburgh's Old Town, a crowded and filthy place that was, Higham writes "a running sore on the prim, gray face of Scotland" (20).

Charles Doyle coped with his failure in two ways. He drank, descending into alcoholism and long periods of despair (Booth 15); eventually he was institutionalized, first in a nursing home for alcoholics, then in an institution for the insane where he died. And he painted. The initial aim may have been to earn extra money, but his "fascination for puerile fairies and elves" was increasingly replaced by "supernatural, nightmarish visions" which grew so "grotesque, melancholic and macabre" that they no longer sold (Booth 8).

If escape into a nightmarish world of the supernatural was Arthur Conan Doyle's inheritance from his father, he took from his mother a passion for romance and history, and the sense that he was something much finer than his impoverished and chaotic life in Edinburgh might suggest. Mary Doyle's obsession was with her own forebears, as she claimed royal blood through her mother's line and Irish aristocracy from Tudor times through her father's. Some of her claims, Booth writes, were "tenuous in the extreme" but her "genealogical fantasies" bolstered her spirits and "instilled in her children a certain pride, fascination and respect for their roots." Mary's partner in this interest was her son Arthur, who "absorbed her stories of knights and heraldry, courage and honour, weaving them into his own childish tales of historical adventure" which became his own "welcome escape into fantasy from his father's descent into dipsomania" (11). His mother's stories of the royal forebears were so intense, Conan Doyle later wrote, that they obscured "the real facts of my life" (qtd. in Stashower 22). As hobbies, the young Conan Doyle took up the study of heraldry, and learned to read genealogical tables. While Mary Doyle thus provided her son with an escape from the harshness of his life, she also seems to have used him, not only, as Booth writes, "as a consolation for the shortcomings of her husband," but also to mirror back her own sense of being better than her surroundings (11).[1]

Conan Doyle's early childhood, with its alternation between the scramble of poverty and an imagined greatness was completed by a Jesuit education in a harsh boarding school beginning at the age of nine, where a message of "moral elitism" (Booth 26) was enforced with severe punishment and "fear and intimidation" (23). Here life was extremely Spartan, with discipline paramount; Conan Doyle was to remember that he was in rebellion against the authoritarian atmosphere and took many beatings: "One blow of [a rubber paddle] delivered with intent, would cause the palm of the hand to swell up and change colour," he later wrote. "To take twice-nine upon a cold day was about the extremity of human endurance" (qtd. in Booth 24). While one of his teachers, Francis Cassidy, was remembered for his kindness and encouragement, he was an exception. The other Jesuits, Booth writes, "repressed their own emotions and stamped on any the boys might have shown . . . their unemotional approach to life had by default driven him to read and escape through books," especially stories of Empire, histories, and historical novels (35).

Neither Conan Doyle's home life nor his school environment appear to have worked to modify grandiose fantasy; instead grandiosity is offered as a compensation for an ever-present sense of loss and fear. Such a breakdown may explain why Conan Doyle most wanted to be known for the triumphalist historical novel, and also why it was the detective stories filled with ordinary people whose lives seemed to be spinning out of control where his real talents lay.

Sherlock Holmes' beginnings do not seem particularly auspicious of the role the detective would soon play in public life: The first Holmes story, "A Study in Scarlet," is a lumbering tale of cultish, polygamous Mormans who carry a feud from America to England. Derivative of both Poe and Stevenson, the story was written quickly with none of the extensive research that went into Conan Doyle's historical novels and was published to minor notice in a Christmas annual of 1887. The character of Holmes, however, thought to have been based on one of Doyle's medical school instructors, was an instant success.

The response to the next story, "The Sign of the Four," was good, but not good enough to stop Conan Doyle, who still earned his living from a limp medical practice, from going to Vienna where he hoped, without much actual prospect of success, to beef up his career by specializing in ophthalmology. But in 1891 press baron George Newnes, who had made a fortune from an early mass circulation magazine, *Tit-bits*, started the *Strand Magazine*, and asked Conan Doyle for six Holmes stories, believing that presentation of a known fictional character in successive, self-contained stories was the best way to build a readership. The first of these Holmes stories, "Scandal in Bohemia," was published in 1891 to overwhelming response. Not only were the stories wildly popular, but it was also apparent that many people had come to believe that Holmes was a real person, and both Conan Doyle and Scotland Yard began to receive letters asking for Holmes' autograph (Booth 178).

The immense popularity of Sherlock Holmes along with the wishful sense that he was both a real person and immortal, hints at the concerns of imperial Britain when its guard is down, as it sinks into stories that are not designed explicitly as imperial propaganda. For, despite the cozy scenes of Holmes in dressing gown and slippers before the fire, the excitement of clattering cabs, and the railway jaunts to fine old country houses, we see, throughout the Sherlock Holmes stories, a country beset by a variety of ills, most of which threaten to undermine the established social order. Though there was an abundance of real crime in late Victorian London, as Stephen Knight writes, Conan Doyle seldom draws professional criminals. An exception, the arch criminal, Professor Moriarity, seems to be introduced primarily as a device to get rid of the detective Conan Doyle had grown weary of (Knight 370).

Rather, an examination of the first thirty eight stories, published from 1888 to 1902, along with the novella *The Hound of the Baskervilles*, reveals that approximately two thirds of the cases are the result not of professional criminal activity, but of some foreign pollution that, like a mysterious disease, has been carried into the country, frequently by returning Britons who have been corrupted during their years abroad. The stories incessantly if indirectly intimate that there is an unwanted corollary to Britain's advance into all corners of the globe.[2] If the dangers in the stories reveal a narcissistic vulnerability, the sense that there is a curse attached to imperial expansion, that it contains within it the seeds of destruction of British life at home, this vulnerability is balanced by a study in grandiosity, the omniscient and omnipotent detective, Sherlock Holmes.

There are several ways in which foreign contamination arrives in England in the Sherlock Holmes stories. In some cases, there is no direct relationship to imperial activities, only a general sense that the purity of England is constantly under assault from foreign sources, generally in the form of unsound personal and political practices. Often, in this type of story, Holmes must solve cases involving foreign quarrels that find their way to England. The first story, "A Study in Scarlet," reflects sensational contemporary reporting of the doings of American Mormons, and turns upon what is shown to be the despicable practice of polygamy. This practice causes a young American woman to be married against her will, and involves the young man who loves her in a quest for revenge which begins in California and finally culminates in England. Other cases of foreign practices threatening the British involve German counterfeiters who have set up in the English countryside but whose schemes require them to kidnap English engineers ("The Adventure of the Engineer's Thumb"), Italian Mafiosi who arrive via America ("The Adventure of the Six Napoleons"), and Russian revolutionists – "nihilists, you understand" – who pursue an informer to England where he has posed for some time as a mild-mannered college professor ("The Adventure of the Golden Pince Nez"). The foreign drugs of heroin or opium are sometimes in the background as facilitators to evil doing, and in one case, "The Naval Treaty," French spies appear to have stolen a critical secret document.

If the stories mentioned above hint of an England constantly undermined by reprehensible foreign schemes and practices, a second set of stories shows a specific link between problems in England and imperial activities. In these there is the sense that the English are in danger of moral degeneration as a result of their experiences in the colonies, or their contact with racial others. Those who have been thus contaminated often return with foreign wealth to England, where they set themselves up in country estates. Eventually, though, they will face retribution for their past deeds, a retribution which often destroys them and their innocent English heirs as well. The stories indicate not only that foreign wealth carries with it a curse, but also that those who return from abroad threaten the stability of English society in its traditional heartland, the countryside, where wealth, land and position are properly acquired through inheritance over generations, not with the proceeds of dubious endeavors in India, Australia, South America or South Africa.

That the true horror in these stories is fear of destruction of the grandiose self can be seen in the attitude expressed toward the dubious activities of the British abroad. We notice that it is usually not the actual crimes of the returning English which are problematic; rather it is the threatened *revelation* of these crimes. As long as these deeds remain secret, the perpetrators may prosper, may even use the resultant gain to set themselves up as respectable members of society. One can live, Conan Doyle suggests, with the knowledge of one's shady activities abroad, as long as these remain secret. But the moment the crime is made known, these characters, who embody the struggle of the grandiose self to suppress the feared inner bad self, simply drop dead.

In one of the stories that explores the theme of Britons contaminated by experiences in other lands, "The Boscombe Valley Mystery," an Englishman, John Turner, has gone to Australia, gotten rich as a highway robber, then returned to England. He buys the largest estate in the area, and lives as a gentleman, raising one daughter. Another Englishman returned from Australia, McCarthy, knows of this criminal past. He blackmails Turner, then schemes to have his own son marry Turner's daughter and inherit his fortune. Turner kills McCarthy, and tries to blame the murder on McCarthy's son. In the end, both older men die, more or less for their sins. The young people, who are themselves innocent of any foreign taint, marry, though the story closes with the note that a "black cloud" hovers over them (*Holmes* 1: 289).

Sometimes, as in "The Gloria Scott," those who have committed evil deeds abroad are not actually destroyed by others, but die of sheer guilty terror when it seems these actions may be revealed. In this story, an Englishman who stole money to pay a "debt of honor," is convicted of theft and transported to Australia. On the voyage to the penal colony, he takes part in a prison ship mutiny; once in Australia, he makes a fortune in the gold fields, returning to buy a country estate in England. When he is visited by men who knew him from his convict days, the horrible prospect that he is soon to be unmasked kills him. In their horror of being found out, these characters resemble those with narcissistic disturbance who alternate between a sense of grandiose dominance and a sense of inner emptiness, loss and depression.

The young lovers in "Boscombe Valley" are given a chance to enjoy the wealth their fathers acquired in the colonies and to escape its curse; the son in "Gloria Scott" can at least try to build a life in exile. And in a story called "The Adventure of the Solitary Cyclist" a young woman escapes the snare of con men who knew her uncle in South Africa where the fortune she is to inherit was made. Other innocent heirs to foreign fortunes, however, are not so lucky. In "The Five Orange Pips," an

Englishman has gone to America, and become a planter. He returns after the Civil War with a fortune, giving as his reason for leaving America "an aversion to negroes and his dislike of the Republican policies in extending the franchise to them" (1: 292). The man, Elias Openshaw, played an important role in the Ku Klux Klan and is, like John Turner, now being threatened by men who knew him abroad. They apparently seek to get papers about clan activities which could incriminate "the first men of the South," and which Openshaw refuses to give up. Not only does Openshaw die mysteriously – also of fright, it is hinted – but his English nephew dies in the same way. In the end Holmes traces the perpetrators to a ship out of Savannah, Georgia. As if in divine retribution for the crime, the ship is lost at sea.

Since the narcissist projects upon others the characteristics of his own exploitive nature, it follows that the more "exploitive" one's attitude toward others, the more dangerous the others may appear to be. Thus, those who return with wealth from the relatively empty spaces of America or Australia are usually shown as lonely misanthropes whose primary activity is to wait gloomily on a remote country estate for their pasts to catch up with them. But those who return from India have been subjected to a more evil foreign influence, and appear to have received a more virulent infection. Often the dangerous influences of the Indian environment have driven them to commit crimes of violence, so that they are also guilty of a more direct and dangerous importation of foreign evil.

In "The Sign of Four," the second Sherlock Holmes story, a complex plot shows Englishmen corrupted and thrown off their moral balance by the commotion and carnage of the "Mutiny," as the 1857 uprising against the British was called, and drawn into crime by Indian associates. In this story an enlisted man, Jonathan Small, is crippled both physically – a crocodile has bitten off his leg – and morally by India. After rehearsing a bit of "Mutiny" horror of burning bungalows and murdered white women, he explains that in the chaos of the "Mutiny," human life had come to seem expendable. In this environment he went along with a murder plot hatched by Indians to kill the servant of a rajah and take the treasure the servant was carrying. The murder was made more palatable by the fact that the rajah was treacherous, having supported both sides in the "Mutiny," and also since the servant was contemptible, fat, fearful and twitching "like a mouse when he ventures from his hole" (1: 193). Small's crime was discovered and prosecuted by British authorities and he was sent to a penal island, where he confided the whereabouts of the stolen treasure to the English in charge, who, as officers and gentlemen, needed money to pay their gambling debts. The officers double-crossed Small and returned with the treasure to England where they lived in luxury, though one of them was accidentally killed as the two quarreled over division of the loot. Eventually Small is helped to escape by a native companion,

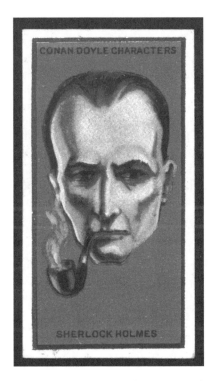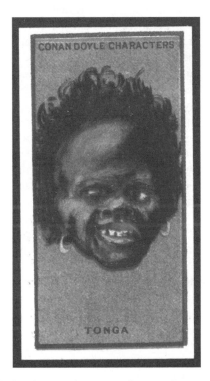

Cigarette cards showing the detective Sherlock Holmes and Tonga, a character from "The Sign of Four." Tonga, a "savage and distorted creature" brought back from India by an English enlisted man, is portrayed as simultaneously venomous and servile. Holmes, by contrast, is elegant, coolly detached, knowledgeable on all subjects, effortlessly superior to professional police and wrong-doers alike.

Tonga, who despite his "venomous" nature is "devoted" to Small. Small ekes out an income in England by exhibiting the devoted Tonga at fairs – "he would eat raw meat and dance his war dance" (203) – until he can find the treacherous officer, Sholto, and the treasure.

If Small is physically and morally deformed by India, Tonga is evil incarnate, so much so that Watson and Holmes, normally reliant upon the damning quality of Holmes' evidence to halt wrong-doers, draw their guns at the very sight of him. He was, Watson reports, in an orgy of horrified disgust, "a little black man – the smallest I have ever seen – with a great, misshapen head and a shock of tangled, disheveled hair. Holmes had drawn his revolver, and I whipped out mine at the sight of this savage, distorted creature . . . that face was enough to give a man a sleepless night. Never have I seen features so deeply marked with all bestiality and cruelty. His small eyes glowed and burned with a somber light, and his thick lips were writhed back from his teeth which grinned and chattered in half animal fury" (178).

Before Small can stop him, Tonga kills Sholto with a poison dart, demonstrating again how association with India and Indians can result in evil-doing which is, however reprehensible, not really all one's fault. This defense appears to be one with which even the stern and disapproving Holmes can nevertheless sympathize:

"I don't believe that I can swing for the job," Small protests. "I give you my word on the book that I never raised hand against Mr. Sholto. It was that little hell-hound, Tonga, who shot one of his cursed darts into him. I had not part in it, sir. I was as grieved as if it had been my blood-relation. I welted the little devil with the slack end of the rope for it, but it was done and I could not undo it again."

"Have a cigar," said Holmes, "and you had best take a pull out of my flask" (180).

Finally, it is in the best-known and longest of the Sherlock Holmes stories, "The Hound of the Baskervilles," that Conan Doyle comes closest to expressing directly the sense of an England beset by a "curse" of empire. The Baskervilles are a fine old family, still imbued with a sense of *noblesse oblige*, still the necessary rock of traditional England. But this representative family is sterile and shaken, reduced to obtaining wealth abroad, an endeavor that *always*, in these stories, results in degradation and guilt, wrecked lives, and an inevitable weakening of the social order that those acquiring the wealth seek to rejoin. The story is a striking example of both the intense fear of moral decay, and also how these fears may finally be projected onto a foreign environment so that the "curse" may be lifted. The story, thus, is a classic of narcissistic ambivalence. The Baskervilles are simultaneously superior to foreigners and the lower classes, and themselves guilty of dark secret evil.

In the story, the Baskervilles, a "good" and "old" family, are said to be cursed, the result of an ancestor, Hugo, who died in drunken pursuit of a farmer's daughter who was also killed. Since then family members have met unusual deaths, and it is said that a giant ghostly hound roams the moors, waiting to take revenge upon new generations. The Baskervilles are shown in serious decay; two brothers, Charles and Rodger, have been forced to go abroad, to South Africa and South America, and the son of a third, deceased brother, has gone to Canada. As the story opens, Charles has returned from South Africa with enough money to restore the family seat, but, as is common to those returning with wealth from abroad, he becomes a virtual recluse in the gloomy old mansion.

Repeatedly in the Sherlock Holmes stories there is the sense that the backbone of the country and of English tradition is found among the old country families, not in metropolitan London. Although urbane, Sherlock Holmes himself is descended from country squires and London is shown in the first Holmes story to be hopelessly polluted from abroad, a "great cesspool into which all the loungers and idlers of Empire" are drained (1: 4). In "The Hound of the Baskervilles," Sir Charles is a gloomy and troubled man; still his restoration of the family estate is shown to be a relief and a boon to the those who live in the surrounding area. He has taken on a paternalistic role toward the neighborhood at large and the local paper reports that "it was his openly expressed desire that the whole countryside should, within his own lifetime, profit by his good fortune . . . his generous donations to local and county charities have been frequently chronicled" (2: 14).

If the old country families thus represent a last bastion of traditional values against a London full of imperial waste, we may consider the troubles of the Baskervilles as the plight of traditional England itself. When Charles Baskerville dies at the end of his own lane, his face distorted with fear, supposedly after a visitation from a giant, spectral hound, we are invited to consider what it is that roams out on the dark moors – and in the darkness of the subconscious – which has frightened him to death. Is it a force bent upon punishing the guilt of his ancestor, Hugo Baskerville? Or is the old legend really a cover for a more immediate situation? One clue that the latter may be the case is that Sir Charles's death of fear is very similar to other such deaths in the Sherlock Holmes stories, deaths which are always brought on by the horror that one's past imperial deeds are about to be revealed. The "hound" of the Baskervilles appears to be the terrifying truth of one's inner iniquity that, when revealed, results in the death of one's grandiose self image, rendered here as the physical death of the character.

In a rather complex maneuver, however, Conan Doyle draws back from finally revealing the deeds which have caused Sir Charles's guilty fear. Rather he brings in a substitute, Sir Charles' brother, Rodger, one highly exposed to foreign contamination, and one who has not sought to retire respectably in the countryside. Rodger has long been in South America where he stole public money, married a local beauty, and then returned to England where he lived by committing burglaries in the countryside. In line to inherit the family estate, Rodger has plotted to frighten Charles to death with a huge dog whose mouth has been made to glow fiendishly with phosphorous. Thus the deeds behind Sir Charles's guilty terror, along with Sir Charles himself, are allowed to vanish discreetly into the darkness, as his brother Rodger, who has not accepted the necessity of upholding British grandiosity, and hiding imperial guilt, is brought forward for blame and punishment.

Tellingly, Rodger does not succeed in his attempt to frighten another heir, the young Sir Henry, to death. Henry has been "farming" in Canada all these years and presumably has not come into contact with wealth, criminal opportunities, exotic beauties or racial others powerful enough to exert a corrupting influence. In the end Sir Henry represents a re-infusion of Anglo-Saxon virtues, which were originally based on an honest relationship with the land, and which have been stored safely away in wholesome young North America – particularly the part of North America with neither plantation wealth nor gold. He seems to provide the best hope for a physical and moral rejuvenation of crumbling old England.

The sense that foreign wealth is cursed and foreign influence destabilizing betrays feelings of emptiness, loss and vulnerability to destruction that are part of the narcissistic equation. Balancing these fears is a grandiose wish for omnipotence found in the near omniscience with which Sherlock Holmes can solve seemingly insoluble problems. Holmes is knowledgeable on all subjects, coolly superior to both professional police and wrong-doers. Finally, the near-magical nature of Holmes' abilities of detection betrays the narcissist fear that such power is not real, but only a fantasy.

If Conan Doyle's historical romances were tepidly received as run-of-the-mill imperial propaganda for children, the modern-day knight as portrayed by Sherlock Holmes, one who could deal quickly and efficiently with the disorder brought about by imperial contact, appears to have spoken directly to the needs of contemporary England.

The qualities which mark Holmes as a gentleman-knight are numerous. Repeatedly we are shown Holmes undertaking his work of detection as a sort of hobby, a kick; for him a good mystery works, like the cocaine with which he injects himself (1: 107). Like the knight in search of a quest, Holmes craves excitement and action, and can not abide the "dull routine of existence," which suffices for ordinary people. As a fantasy of narcissistic grandiosity, Holmes is not just everyknight, but unique in his desire for daring deeds: "I crave mental exaltation," he explains in "The Sign of Four." "That is why I have chosen my own particular profession or rather created it, for I am the only one in the world" (1: 108). Unlike the professional man, who is limited to a narrow range of concerns, Holmes is interested in all that which is "bizarre and outside the conventions and humdrum routine of everyday life" (230). Indeed, his life is "one long effort to escape from the commonplaces of existence" (251). When he is not thrilling to battle, Holmes is arranged in postures of aristocratic lassitude. We see him "lounging in his sitting room in his dressing gown" where he rests with a glass of brandy and water, gazing into his fire, and reaching for his violin, noting that his only real problem is not the mystery at hand but "how to while away these bleak autumnal evenings" (407). As an aristocratic hobbyist, Holmes is repeatedly at pains to distinguish himself from his professional counterparts. When Roylott, the son of an old Saxon family who has gone bad in India, visits Holmes and hurls at him a number of insults, Holmes takes offense only at one of the man's remarks: "Fancy his having the insolence to confound me with the official detective force!" (357).

That Conan Doyle himself saw Holmes as a 19th century version of a medieval knight is clear from these lines found in one of the earliest stories, "The Sign of Four."

"It's a romance," cries a woman, upon hearing about a case Holmes and Watson are pursuing. "An injured lady, half a million in treasure, a black cannibal, and a wooden legged ruffian. They take the place of the conventional dragon or wicked earl."

"And two knight errants to the rescue," adds another woman (1: 164).

As a gentleman dilettante Holmes is expert in a number of areas of study. Some of his interests, upon which he can speak knowledgeably "as if he has made a special study" of the subject (172), include miracle plays, medieval pottery, Stradivarius violins, the Buddhism of Ceylon, and the warships of the future. He is a violinist, and "a composer of no ordinary merit," reads medieval texts, is quick with quotes from Goethe, Flaubert, and Georges Sand, and knows how to order a "quiet Epicurean little cold supper" when entertaining a lord.

Both the aristocrat and the knight sometimes go masked so as not to be bound by the conventions of identity that restrict ordinary people, and Holmes is a genius of disguise, often appearing to become the character he seeks to portray: "It was not merely that Holmes changed his costume," Watson remarks. "His expression, his manner, his very soul seemed to vary with every fresh part that he assumed. The stage lost a fine actor . . . when he became a specialist in crime" (1: 223). Not only can Holmes assume any disguise, but in a way reminiscent of Rudyard Kipling's *Kim*, published a few years earlier, he is quick to take charge in any foreign land he may visit. This is shown when Holmes spends several years traveling. He went to Tibet, he reports, "and amused myself by visiting Lassa, and spending some days with the head lama. . . . I then passed through Persia, looked in at Mecca, and paid a short but interesting visit to the Khalifa at Khartoun, the results of which I have communicated to the Foreign Office. Returning to France, I spent some months in a research into the coal tar derivatives, which I conducted in a laboratory at Montpellier" (1: 670).

I have suggested that Conan Doyle may have disliked his famous creation because the Sherlock Holmes stories betrayed the sense of loss and dislocation that is the underside of grandiose fantasy, a loss and dislocation Conan Doyle was at pains to deny in his own life. It may also have been that Holmes, for all his cool omniscience, is not, finally, omniscient enough for Conan Doyle, whose later works betray a desire for knowledge and control that goes beyond the boundaries of 19th century experience, even of human life itself. Holmes' powers were only temporal. Increasingly, Conan Doyle aspired to reach beyond this life, to contact the dead to receive reports from them on the nature of the afterlife and the future of the world.

In the 1911 book, *The Lost World,* Conan Doyle disdains the "conquest of one nation by another" that had interested him in *The White Company*; now his band of Englishmen wipe out not a nation but an entire species, exterminating the last members of a race of pre-historic "ape men" that have survived in the wilds of South America. As the ape-men are gruesomely destroyed, Professor Challenger, who leads the expedition, exults at having been present at one of the battles which will determine "the fate of the world." Wars between nations are "meaningless," he declares, but the fights to determine which species rules "were the victories that count" (207).

The desire for racial dominance and the fantasy of racial genocide is obvious in this story. But there is another theme that will be of increasing importance to Conan Doyle in the years after World War I, the desire to win acceptance for spiritualist beliefs, notions that were widely considered either absurd or fraudulent. Professor Challenger, who has been ridiculed for proposing that pre-historic creatures exist and who has even been accused – as Conan Doyle will also be accused – of faking photographs of phenomena that falls beyond the knowledge of science, has the satisfaction of bringing a pterodactyl back to England and displaying it in a lecture hall to astound and confound his critics. Finally, in an undisguised fantasy of grandiose triumph, the professor's brilliant prescience is acknowledged and he and the other explorers are carried out into the street where they are met with a "roar of acclamation" from a hundred thousand people who tie up traffic in central London for hours as they cheer and sing "They are Jolly Good Fellows" (242).

As Professor Challenger devotes his life to proving beliefs that fly in the face of science, Arthur Conan Doyle would, in the years during and after World War I, become a "ferocious and evangelistic propagandist" of spiritualism (Booth 315). He was not alone in these beliefs; many sought to deal with the unprecedented scale of death experienced in World War I through the hope that the dead could be contacted. But though the fad for spiritualism faded in the years that followed the war, Conan Doyle became even more determined to win acceptance for his beliefs, writing numerous books and articles and lecturing around the world. He held séances where he claimed to contact, among others, Cecil Rhodes, who communicated through automatic writing, and his mother, who apologized for the skepticism of spiritualism she had expressed when alive. And he was widely mocked for supporting the validity of photographs which seemed to reveal the unseen presence of spirits and fairies, effects which were shown to be easily reproducible in a dark room.

Increasingly irritated by the skepticism with which his views were met, Conan Doyle claimed in 1924 to have information from the spirit world about the nature of the world's end, and once claimed he had received "eight-seven separate forecasts of doom." Though supported in his beliefs by his second wife Jean, whom he married upon the death of his first wife, Conan Doyle was widely ridiculed and satirized, and many friends viewed him "either as an embarrassment, an enigma or a harmless but vociferous crackpot" (Booth 334).

The peculiarity of so many of Conan Doyle's causes bring one to puzzle again over how a man of such irrational notions could create the most rational of characters. One way of viewing the Holmes stories may be that they were created in part by the British public itself, whose hunger for neat solutions to complex problems protected the crusty know-it-all from the ire of his creator and kept the detective alive through scores of adventures. In an age growing increasingly insecure, Holmes is a modern day knight, hungry for romantic adventure, one to whom dominance is second nature. He seems to speak to a fear that the mundane minds of professionals are unequipped to protect England against the new and nearly fantastical menace washing in every day from a variety of bizarre lands and cultures. For this, England needs a new kind of knight, one with wide ranging interests, whose desire for adventure propels him into imaginative solutions which can undo these threats. Holmes's fantastic abilities and unfailing superiority guarantee eventual triumph over all challenges, an unquestionable superiority that may have been so attractive precisely because it is an attitude the British fear they may be losing.

5 RUDYARD KIPLING

Black Sheep

"Aunty Rosa had the power to beat him with many stripes. It was unjust and cruel and Mamma and Papa would never have allowed it. Unless perhaps, as Aunty Rosa seemed to imply, they had sent secret orders. In which case he was abandoned indeed." RUDYARD KIPLING

From the time his book of short stories set in India, *Plain Tales from the Hills*, was published in 1888, Rudyard Kipling's importance to the imperial project was immense; perhaps more than any other writer he created the late 19th century idea of empire. Cecil Rhodes, who became Kipling's close friend and benefactor, praised him for showing the world the strength of British rule (Angus Wilson 224) and the *Morning Post* editorialized that Kipling "contributed more than anyone, perhaps, toward the consolidation of British Empire" (215).

This is the Kipling with which we are most familiar, the leading poet of imperialism, remembered for such phrases as "the white man's burden." His early works, however, come as a surprise, for in them we find very little to suggest confident, effective imperial rule and a great many scenes of frightened and fundamentally helpless young men struggling to survive in a world of disorientation and futility.

In these stories, we do not yet see anything like the young English god and adoring, slavish natives whom we will encounter in later works such as *Kim*, nor do we see the full unleashing of narcissistic rage seen in stories such as "A Sahib's War," where enemies are portrayed as bestial sub-humans and where the narration flirts with fantasies of torture. Rather, these early stories focus on the gap between imperial ideology and reality, a gap that is filled by the bodies of hot, miserable, and rather rudderless young men: "Recruities sometimes cry, an' sometime they don't know fwat they do, an' sometime they are all for cuttin' throats an' such like dhirtiness; but some men get heavy-dead-dhrunk on the fightin" (*Soldiers* 56).

Perhaps it is for this reason that Kipling was well known to American GIs during the Vietnam war. Dexter Jeffries writes, "He seemed to be the only who knew anything about the perils awaiting those who were put down where empire placed its paw." As a result, Jeffries says, "we all knew the lines from this poem":

And the end of the fight is a tombstone white
With the name of the late deceased
And the epitaph drear: 'A Fool likes here
Who tried to hustle the East.'

The GIs "regarded the idiots in Washington as just another in the series of those who tried 'to hustle the East,'" Jeffries says.[1]

As Kipling repeatedly constructs portraits of lost and struggling young men in these early stories, he resembles patients described by Alice Miller, people who work to heal themselves by replaying their experiences of loss, instinctively, often unconsciously, trying to grasp the source of their depression or feelings of emptiness. There is, to be sure, a great deal of self-pity in Kipling's first two collections of short stories, as well as a pronounced under-current of revenge fantasy. But the wish for revenge is controlled, and self-pity is quite different from the grandiosity alternating with depression and rage of the full-fledged narcissist. Kipling's work is not completed here, and as we read forward we can trace the trajectory from the hurt child, still struggling to understand his experience, to the full-fledged narcissist, no longer able to grapple honestly with his own loss, but fluctuating between grandiosity, and a sense of emptiness and narcissistic rage.

If we are to read Kipling as in some way departing from the usual imperial line, we must be careful to understand the nature of this departure. It surely was not the intention of the very young Kipling, aged seventeen when he began his writing career in India, to consciously oppose empire; indeed his letters home show a young man intent upon reinforcing key tenants of imperial belief for those at home. Writing to his cousin Margaret Burne-Jones from Lahore in January of 1886, for example, he responds to her question whether the English have the "welfare of the natives much at heart" in the affirmative; if she had met some of the men he has met, he writes, she would "cross out the sentence" questioning British motives "and weep. What else are we working in the country for. For what else do the best men of the Commission die from overwork, and disease, if not to keep the people alive in the first place and healthy in the second. We spend our best men on the country like water and if ever a foreign country was made better through 'the blood of the martyrs,' India is that country" (Pinney 98).

Even here, however, Kipling is unable to avoid seeing two aspects of empire that will become central themes of his early fiction: the suffering of the young men charged with carrying out imperial work, and the sense of the uselessness of British actions despite the "martyrdom" of its men: "Underneath our excellent administrative system, under the piles of reports and statistics; the thousands of troops; the doctors . . . runs wholly untouched and unaffected the life of the peoples of the land – a life as full of impossibilities and wonders as the Arabian Nights. . . . Our rule, so long as no one steals too flagrantly or murders too openly, affects it in no way whatever" (99).

Zoreh Sullivan, in her study *Narratives of Empire: The Fictions of Rudyard Kipling*, speculates upon the reasons for the sense of "loss and horror" in the early stories, writing that, "It is easy" to explain these, "in terms of English education" of "Kipling's childhood, or a system that victimized its children in schools that concealed ruthlessness with rigidity and discipline." But, she argues, the stories, "refuse to allow such single explanations for events that signify multiple possibilities of competing political, social and psychological meanings" (110).

Yet, I suggest that there may also be a deceptive ease in using the teenage Kipling to reflect contemporary concepts, as Sullivan in her Lacanian reading, speculates that Kipling's "fascination" with psychic "breakdown" is his "way of internalizing the unacceptable terror of anni-hilation or boundary slippage in the troubling structures of gender, race and identity" (79). Further, such an explanation does not help us to under-stand how it is that one very young and in many ways conventional man apprehends the "troubling structures of gender, race and identity" which elude others of his class.

I will contend that as Charles Dickens' early experience of being put to work in a boot blacking plant allowed him to see and identify with the misery of the poor in London with an intensity that many other writers of the time could not, Kipling's experience of psychic and even physical torture at a very early age allows him to grasp, on some level, the hypocrisy that can lie at the heart of self-righteous authority. In these first stories we see Kipling reading empire not entirely through the lens of accepted ideology – though he pays dutiful lip service to this ideology – but in large part through that of his own experience, that of a young person left to fend for himself in conditions that verged upon the desperate. While it may well be, as Sullivan suggests, that childhood trauma is not the "only explanation" for the "loss and horror" found in the early stories, it is surely one vital piece of the puzzle.

Even by child-rearing standards of the day, Kipling's early experience was extreme. As set out in the autobiographical story, "Baa Baa, Black Sheep," and the autobiographical novel, *The Light That Failed*, confirmed in Kipling's autobiography, *Something of Myself*, and verified by his sister Trix, between the ages of five to eleven Kipling was subjected to psychic and even physical torture, as, in the absence of his parents, who had deposited the children in England and returned to India, a paid caregiver devoted herself to stripping him of every shred of comfort, pleasure or self-respect.

To understand the trauma the young Kipling experienced during this time, we must first look at his life from birth to five years, when his situation seems to have supported and probably unhealthily prolonged primary narcissism. Born in India, he was cared for by native servants, and taken everywhere by them in a world that seems, in his memory, to be full of beauty, light and benevolence. His first impression, he writes, in *Something of Myself*, is of "daybreak, light and colour and golden and purple fruits at the level of my shoulder. This would be the memory of early morning walks to the Bombay fruit market with my *ayah*. . . . Meeta, my Hindu bearer, would sometimes go into little Hindu temples where, being below the age of caste, I held his hand and looked at the dimly seen, friendly Gods" (3).

If the world, as presented by the child's servants, is full of light and beauty, the servants themselves, as shown in Kipling's memory, feed the infant sense that all exists for his pleasure, and do little to help the child accept the need to balance one's own desires with the wishes of others. The little English boy portrayed in the autobiographical story, "Baa Baa, Black Sheep," is "the unquestioned despot of . . . Bombay" (Raine 93).[2] When the story's young protagonist Punch commands his *ayah* to keep telling stories, even though it is bedtime, and even though more stories will wake his little sister, she obeys. Parents are not always so easy to command, but in Kipling's case parents do not seem to have been much present. Though the mother is remembered singing at the piano before going out to dinner, and the father, who was a professor of architecture at an industrial design school in Bombay, is recalled drawing funny pictures, they did not spend enough time with the child to make English his first language. In his memoir, Kipling recounts being dressed and taken into the dining room to see his parents, of being admonished to "speak English to Papa and Mamma," and of struggling to translate "out of the vernacular idiom that one thought and dreamed in" (*Something* 4). In "Baa Baa, Black Sheep," it is his *ayah* who first hints that that the little boy is going away to England, and she alone expresses sadness at his departure (Raine 88).

From an early childhood, which seems to have fed the child's infant grandiosity, and to have done little to help him modify narcissistic desires, Kipling, along with his three-year-old sister, was taken to England and entrusted to a stranger. It was customary to return Anglo-Indian children to England once infancy was passed, and Kipling's parents were only complying with this practice. Even so, their method of introducing the children to this change seems shocking in its insensitivity. Without any explanation or preparation, the parents slipped away in the night and the children awoke to find themselves in the care of a strange woman, Sarah Holloway, whom the children were told to call "Auntie Rosa," and who had been hired through a newspaper advertisement. If Kipling's early care-givers appear to have fed the child's infant grandiosity and to have done little to help him modify narcissistic desires, now "Aunty Rosa," a woman whose apparent sadism was buoyed by her sense of Christian righteous-ness, seems to have taken it as her task to destroy every fragment of self-esteem in the boy from India, to make his life, Kipling wrote, one of "punishments and humiliation – above all humiliation" (*Something* 8). When the boy in "Baa Baa, Black Sheep" tries to escape into books, he is forbidden to read. His little sister is told not to speak to him because he is bad, a "black sheep." The boy was constantly caned and cuffed by "Auntie Rosa" and her son, interrogated and hounded into minor incon-sistencies, and sent to school with the sign "liar" sewn to the back of his jacket. The boy in the story suffers so much that he thinks of ways to die. When he is told that the paint on toys is poisonous, he promptly goes to the nursery and sucks the paint off all the animals in a play Noah's arc.

The children, as recounted both by Kipling and his sister Alice, called Trix, who in later years suffered a series of psychological breakdowns, had no idea why they had been deposited in this house. The only expla-nation given by "Auntie Rosa" was that they were too much trouble for their parents. The children, both under six years old, were unable to understand, his sister would later remember, "why our parents had deserted us. We had no preparation or explanation; it was like a double death, or rather, like an avalanche that had swept away everything happy and familiar" (qtd. in Edmund Wilson 88).

Though there were well-to-do relatives nearby in England, none seem to have detected the problem and though Rudyard visited them occa-sionally, he did not complain of his situation. Later in his life he explained: "Badly-treated children have a clear notion of what they are likely to get if they betray the secrets of a prison house before they are clear of it" (*Something* 11).

Finally a visitor to "Aunty Rosa's" seemed to have grasped that there was something wrong and contacted the children's mother who returned from India. When, returning, she bent over her son, he "flung up an arm to guard off the cuff that [he] had been trained to expect" (*Something* 12). In "Baa Baa, Black Sheep," the returning mother is portrayed as loving and sympathetic, and the reunion joyful "as if she had never gone." Once again the child feels that he is loved. Still, Kipling's young protagonist notes, "when young lips have drunk deep of the bitter waters of Hate, Suspicion, and Despair, all the Love in the world will not wholly take away that knowledge" (Raine 110).

The portrait drawn here is of a child who has suffered an immense psychological trauma and who seems not to have had – not in India,

Illustrations made by Rudyard Kipling for the autobiographical story, "Baa Baa, Black Sheep," first published in *The Week's News*, Allahabad, 1888, and depicting scenes from the house of a hired caretaker where Kipling and his sister – ages five and three, and called Punch and Judy in the story – were left for five years by their parents who had returned to India.

The boy lying on his stomach is Punch. He is reading but, as Kipling writes in the story, reading has been forbidden so Punch bangs a chair on the floor to make it sound as if he is playing with toys. The caption on the far right reads, "It was not a charming employ for he had to make a playful noise." The ruse is discovered by the caretaker, "Auntie Rosa," who is shown rushing in at the top of the sketch with a bundle of switches. Kipling's caption reads, "'If you're old enough to that,' she said – her Temper was always worse after dinner – ['] you're old enough to be beaten.'"

At top left stands Auntie Rosa's son, Harry, who also speaks disdainfully to Punch. The caption reads, "'You're a liar – a young liar,' said Harry with great conviction, [']and you're to have tea down here because you're not fit to speak to us.[']"

"'Auntie Rosa likes me more than she does you,[']" Punch's little sister Judy tells him at the bottom of the page as the boy sits with his head in his hands. "[']She says that you are a Trial and a Black Sheep and I'm not to speak to you more than I can help.'"

certainly not in England – the necessary assistance in mediating infant narcissism into a healthy relationship with the outer world. Thus begins the career of the man whose vision of the British imperial role will resonate more powerfully than any other with the English public.

Kipling was next sent to a boarding school for the children of colonials which, as the portrait he will later paint in the novel *Stalky and Co.* suggests, had the usual amount of bullying and degradation. Still for Kipling, school appears to have been an improvement over Auntie Rosa's in that he had companions, and the schoolboy threesome portrayed in *Stalky and Co.* who band together for protection and comfort in a hostile world, bears a distinct resemblance to the "soldiers three" of his later stories of imperial India.

At sixteen Kipling went back to India, where his parents had found him a position on a small English language newspaper. For the next seven years he worked as a journalist, doing the many tasks required at small publications. Despite long bouts of insomnia and other illnesses, he wrote much of the copy, including dozens of short stories which appeared in the paper, and would later be collected as *Plain Tales from the Hills* and *Soldiers Three,* first published in 1888 and in 1890, catapulting him into literary fame.

Several clear and related themes emerge from these stories. *Plain Tales,* set in a British hill station to which officers and their families retire from the heat of the plains, is full of mildly comic accounts of hapless, often foolish young men, men who have little idea what they're doing in India, whose sense of how social and romantic affairs should be handled has broken down in the odd new environment, and who, when possible, offer themselves to be managed by usually older, more mature women. Also in these stories, however, and dominating *Soldiers Three,* is the underside of this comic rendering of post-adolescent male confusion, the portrait of young men driven nearly mad by heat, boredom, and fear. Their sole salvation is in the loyalty of their comrades in suffering. The three soldiers of the second book's title must talk each other out of suicide, get each other out of scrapes, listen to each other's laments of lost love and home, and carry each other off to some secret spot where they can smoke and talk each other down from panic. In these stories the young men who theoretically do the work of empire are portrayed as lost boys, trying to get by with the help of friends.

It is difficult to find in the stories the sense that the English are serving any noble or even useful purpose by their presence in India; mostly they are trying to survive. Men may fight bravely, but they are usually motivated by a personal reason that has little to do with the work of empire. In "With the Main Guard," Irish soldiers fight ferociously but only to revenge their own: "They had seen their dead and wanted to kill ivery sowl on the ground" (*Soldiers* 56) In "In the Matter of a Private," a soldier, Simmons, cracks under the strain of heat and heckling and shoots a major, known as Jerry Blazes. Another soldier, Slane, risks his life to rescue the major. Though Slane is hailed as a hero, he is quick to state that his actions were strictly self-serving; he wanted to be lent army horses for his wedding: "Wot did I do it for? For the 'orses o' course . . . Jerry Blazes? If I 'adn't wanted something, Sim might ha' blowed Jerry Blazes' bloomin' 'ead into Hirish stew for aught I'd 'a' cared" (*Soldiers* 68).

To be sure there are figures in these early stories who try to do good work. But even the most dedicated and hard-working men see their efforts come to naught. In "Wressley of the Foreign Office," for example, the civil servant who "knows more about [India] than any living man" (*Plain* 261) writes the best book about Indian history that had ever been written. However, the book fails to impress the young woman Wressley loves, and no one else appears to be interested; he throws away the copies he's had printed and returns to serve out his days as a "report-writing hack" (264).

In the story "Tods' Amendment," officials take note when they learn that a land reform scheme they are planning is viewed by the natives as ridiculous, insulting and unworkable. But if the story paints British administrators as desiring to do right, it also paints them as completely in the dark about native views; they only learn of the natives' disaffection with their plan from a vernacular-speaking six-year-old, Tods, who spends his time with servants and has thus overheard the natives' bitter complaints (*Plain* 182).

In the story "Thrown Away," Kipling shows that it can be misguided and even dangerous to take the work of empire seriously. Here, an earnest young man is driven to suicide because he does not understand that, in India, "Good work does not matter, because a man is judged by his worst output, and another man takes all the credit of his best as a rule. Bad work does not matter, because other men do worse, and incompetents hang on longer in India than anywhere else . . . the wisest thing is to escape as soon as ever you can to some place where amusement is amusement and a reputation worth having" (*Plain* 43).

In much popular imperial writing, a great deal of effort is made to show that any failure of morals and morale among the English in India is finally India's fault, that the fundamentally upright British have been "infected with the corruption and venality endemic in the 'nature' of India" (Castle 17). This is the message, for example, of Arthur Conan Doyle, whose Sherlock Holmes mysteries frequently turn on the problem of returning Englishmen, who have been tainted by their experiences in India, Africa or South America. But here Kipling shows no such thing. Rather it is the senselessness and hopelessness of the British project itself, and his own role in it, which causes Kipling's young protagonist to kill himself.

But the hypocrisy does not end with death, as the suicide must be covered up; those back in England can't be allowed to glimpse the reality behind the facade of empire, even though it is they who have sent the young man out. In a move that makes us think again of Kipling's letters to his cousin in England, those who find the body agree to suppress the truth to reassure those at home. It was, they understand, "utterly impossible to let the letter [the young man has written, describing his sufferings] go Home" (*Plain* 47). In a remarkable snapshot of the terms that those in India are required to accept, the officer who finds the body cuts off one of his own dark curls to send home to the grieving mother, as the young man's own head and hair have been blown to bits by the self-inflicted shotgun blast. Somewhere, the story suggests, there must be a loving mother who would grieve for his suffering if only she knew. But she cannot know, for the arrangements of those in power could be disrupted if such knowledge were allowed to pass. And what must be suppressed, even here, is that the mother too continues to be subtly complicit in sending the boy to his destruction.

Kipling's obsession in these stories is not with what empire does to those who are ruled, but what it does to those charged with the nigh impossible task of ruling. Still, the natives who appear in this early work are seldom shown as having been uplifted by the British presence, and often seem to be victims of the same careless hypocrisy as the young British men. In "Lispeth," a native girl is taken and "civilized" by Christians who then break her heart and bring about her death by lying to her for what they take to be her own good. In "The Story of Muhammad Din," a precocious little Muslim boy, a bold "little man," is distraught when the elaborate mud structures he has lovingly built in an Englishman's garden are heedlessly trampled; the boy is told falsely that the Sahib has intentionally destroyed his work. The Englishman, when he finds out, is sorry and tells the child he may play all he likes. The boy goes back to his work, but, as if to indicate how profound is the cost of a child's shattered belief in the benevolence of the world, he is soon reported dead.

In these stories the work of Britain in India can't be mistaken for a glorious undertaking. Some administrators may mean well; the common soldiers may accept their lot with humor and camaraderie. But despite these efforts, and despite the high price in suffering, little is accomplished.

After publication of *Plain Tales* and *Soldiers Three*, the twenty-four-year-old Kipling returned to London, where he was immensely lionized and immensely depressed. Despite "instant literary success," he felt "increasingly uncertain about his position in England and his status as an 'English' writer" (Ricketts 152). Temporarily without funds despite his success, he lived in squalid rooms. Failing to renew a romance with a young woman for whom he had been carrying a torch in India, he appeared to suffer some sort of psychological breakdown. "I have broken up," he writes to a friend. "My head has given out and I am forbidden work and I am to go away somewhere . . . I must go on alone now till the end of my time. I can do nothing to save myself from breaking up now and again" (qtd. in Ricketts 158).

It was during this period that Kipling wrote the novel, *The Light That Failed*, with its portrait of a deeply depressed young man who resembles Kipling in many ways. Like Kipling, the book's hero, Dick, has spent his youth in a brutal foster home that has left him "savage in soul" (9). Like Kipling, Dick has become a publishing sensation as his drawings of scenes in the Near East have "caught on" with the newspaper reading public. But the acclaim Dick faces when he returns to England is experienced as a sort of assault, corresponding to the sense of the narcissistically damaged person that great success is inevitably followed by a "sense of emptiness and futility, even of shame and anger" if that success is "above all . . . the substitute satisfaction of old needs for echoing, mirroring, and being seen and understood" (Miller *Drama* 43).

Rather than basking in acclaim, Dick feels robbed and unappreciated; his publishers are shown as exploitive, and his fans do not care about him as an artist, only craving more exotic stories to titillate them as they sit cozily with their newspapers and their cups of tea. In response, Dick expresses his contempt for the England to which he has returned. He cannot feel that it is his home, and sees his countrymen's interest in empire as part of the "blind, brutal, British public's bestial thirst for blood" (*Light* 48). He yearns to leave England, and in the following passage we see a fantasy of escape to a setting that sounds much like the Bombay of his childhood, a place where "you can hear the fat coconuts falling from the palms; and you order an ivory-white servant to sling you a long yellow hammock with tassels on it like ripe maize, and you put up your feet and hear the bees hum and the water fall till you go to sleep" (77). Once again, those in power in Britain, indeed the British public itself, are shown to be hypocritical, cruel, and driven by lusts which cause them to destroy earnest and sensitive young people. Placed against this is a fantasy land of gentle, obedient servants, and a yearning to sink back into magical infancy, to be gently rocked to sleep.

As the infant Mohammed Din dies following the destruction of his little world by careless authority, Dick, who has been destroyed by the thoughtless British public, must also die. An old wound, received when he was covering a battle in the Sudan, leads to blindness. Like Kipling, Dick is also rejected by the woman whose love he believes might have saved him and, rather than live on in loveless darkness, he makes his way back to the Sudan, there to re-join soldier friends. These men, like the young soldiers in India, can only try to support one another in the midst of the maddening, meaningless mission upon which they have been sent. In the midst of the horror of battle, Dick imagines that he is back in his foster home, before dying in the arms of a comrade.

Once again, it is impossible to read Kipling as an apologist for or even a supporter of empire. Rather, empire is a show for the British public which is willing to sacrifice its young men either in the name of unattainable ideals or simply to have its appetite for violence and adventure vicariously satisfied. And while these young men cultivate an attitude of cool cynicism in the face of danger, they are not heroes. They are fundamentally passive, suffering figures, holding on to one another, struggling to survive the position into which they have been cruelly thrust.

This is not the last to be heard of a man who would write prolifically until his death in 1936. Nine years later, in 1899, Kipling would publish the poem "The White Man's Burden," in which America is exhorted to sacrifice its young men for the benefit of its ungrateful – "new-caught sullen" – subjects in the Philippines. To a reader of the early work, the shift in Kipling's outlook comes as a shock. For now it is claimed quite clearly, and apparently without irony, that heroic and committed young Anglo-Saxon men should sacrifice themselves entirely for the benefit of those wild and helpless peoples whom they rule. The lines are well known:

> Take up the White Man's burden –
> Send forth the best ye breed –
> Go bind your sons to exile
> To serve your captives' need:
> To wait in heavy harness
> On fluttered folk and wild –
> Your new-caught sullen peoples,
> Half-devil and half-child. (*Gunga* 52)

It must be noted that, in one respect, the poem is similar to Kipling's early work. The young man of empire is faced with a wearying, and in the end nearly impossible task, his efforts "brought to nought" through all the "thankless years." Yet, strikingly, the cause of his misery has changed. Previously the young soldiers and colonials were the victims of the confusion and ineptitude of imperial policy, of heat, hysteria and fear, of the blood lust of the British public. The natives appeared almost incidentally, and sometimes were even represented as fellow sufferers. Now, however, the pain and futility of empire is not largely, as the early stories imply, of British making but entirely the fault of the "slothful" native. The poem's third stanza makes the case:

> Take up the White Man's burden –
> The savage wars of peace –
> Fill full the mouth of Famine
> And bid the sickness cease;
> And when your goal is nearest
> The end for others sought,

Watch Sloth and heathen Folly
Bring all your hope to naught.

This is the Kipling that the world knows, the hatefully racist and conde-
scending champion of the worst of empire. But what has happened
between 1891 and 1899 to occasion this extreme shift?

Let us go back to 1891 when *The Light That Failed*, with its contempt
for the home-bound English public and their thirst for sensational foreign
news, was published. The author, despite his fame and prosperity, was
depressed and in a low state of health, furious at London, the British, and
his publishers (Carrington 121). At this time his agent and beloved friend
Wolcott Balestier died suddenly, and Kipling, just as suddenly, married
Balestier's sister, Carrie. The Balestiers were American and Carrie was a
competent and protective woman a little older than Kipling, who, it would
be widely reported throughout their long marriage, undertook, without
opposition, to manage every aspect of her husband's life. "She guarded
his health," a frequent visitor to the Kiplings would later write, "assumed
the supervision of every detail of the routine of his daily life, published his
works, was his business agent, and stood between him and any obstacles
to the free and full development of his powers" (qtd. in Ricketts 216).

The couple left England and after traveling in Asia and the western
United States settled and built a house on Balestier family property in
Vermont. Kipling's early reports from America seem to show that he felt
he had found the generous, welcoming environment for which he had
longed, something far different from the devouring England he had
encountered both times he had returned there. Surprisingly for the man
who would become the world's best known poet of racism, even the ethnic
mix of America seemed to be part of its merit: "They be the biggest, finest,
and best people on the surface of the globe!" he wrote in *American Notes*.
"Wait till the Anglo-American-German-Jew – the Man of the Future – is
properly equipped. He'll have just the least little kink in his hair now and
again; he'll carry the English lungs above the Teuton feet that can walk
for ever; and he will wave long, thin, bony Yankee hands . . . from one
end of the earth to the other. . . . My heart has gone out to them beyond
all other peoples" (193). And Britons' attitudes toward their country,
which he describes as narrow, selfish and cynical, are compared unfavor-
ably to the deeply-held patriotism of the American. The British
householder sees his country as "an abstraction to supply him with police
and fire brigades"; and the cockney would "laugh in your face" at the
idea that he owes a duty to his land. By contrast, Kipling writes, the
Americans "believe in their land and its future, and its honor and its glory
and they are not ashamed to say so" (*Notes* 237).

At this point in his life Kipling appears not to have descended into
narcissistic fantasy as completely as he will do in later works. Rather he

seems to have sought escape from the invitations to grandiosity, rage, panic and depression that offered themselves in London by setting up a situation that to some extent replicated his happy infancy in India. In the benevolent countryside of Vermont, far from fan and publisher alike, Kipling felt peaceful and protected, with his managing older wife as a replica of the child's loving *ayah*. As Bombay is remembered in Kipling's memoir as a place of "daybreak, light and color," so Vermont is described as a place of light, health, and safety: "The sun and the air and the light are good in this place," he writes in a letter, "and have made me healthy as I never was in my life. . . . It's three miles from anywhere and wondrous self-contained. No one can get at you" (qtd. in Carrington 164).

The couple settled into a farmworker's house on the Balestier's estate which they called Bliss Cottage. There, Kipling wrote almost forty years later in *Something of Myself*, he and Carrie were "extraordinarily and self-centredly content." Looking back, Kipling imagines himself as a safe and cozy infant, remembering hearing "sleigh-bells" that "rang over the white world that tucked us in" as "we counted ourselves secure. . . . We envied no one" (66).

The light and peace of Vermont, and the hopefulness of a forward-looking America, was made even more blissful by the impending arrival of his first child, and the construction of a home which, Kipling wrote, rode "on its hillside like a little boat" (qtd. Ricketts 197). Here Kipling continued to imaginatively revisit his childhood in a little-known story called "The Potted Princess," published in September of 1892, which as Ricketts has noted, is a "radical re-writing" of his childhood history. Rather than being sent off to England at the ages of five and three as were Rudyard and Trix, and as were the children, Punch and Judy, in "Baa Baa, Black Sheep," the children in "The Potted Princess," also Punch and Judy, have not been sent away at all. Rather they remain in India at the ages of seven and five, happy and loved by servants and parents. It is, Ricketts writes, the picture of a "restored" child, as though the traumatic years at Mrs. Holloway's house "had never happened or been miraculously cancelled out" (195).

The revisionist plot of "The Potted Princess" suggests that in the security of his marriage and his home tucked away from the world, Kipling has been able to fantasize a safe and happy childhood. Then, in the two *Jungle Books* written at this time, Kipling does something even more significant and potentially healing, allowing his boy hero, Mowgli, to mourn the loss of childhood security in stories that contain, as Ricketts, shows, a "repeated pattern of abandonment." It is impossible, Miller writes, to return to a "paradise of preambivalent harmony." But through mourning what was lost, the adult can return to his own "world of feelings" and escape the extremes of narcissistic grandiosity and despair (*Drama* 15).

The stories portray the boy Mowgli who is raised among jungle animals with whom he lives in innocent bliss; as he matures, however, and his difference from them becomes apparent, he is cast out and forced to return to the world of men. But there too he is different, and he is cast out once again. Like Kipling, torn from his loving Indian servants, at home neither in India nor England, Mowgli has no place. While the boy in "Baa Baa, Black Sheep," simply suffers, Mowgli grasps the nature of his grief: He sings, "The Jungle is shut to me and the village gates are shut. Why?" (97). Though there are, to be sure, moments of grandiosity that hint of what is to come in *Kim*, Mowgli, very much unlike Kim, is also able to openly mourn his outcast state, crying "as though his heart would break" (53).

But like India and England before it, America proved a cruel betrayer. First, familiarity had taken the bloom off of Kipling's romance with America, and Kipling now criticized his new home to William Henley: "The moral dry rot of it all is having no law that need be obeyed: no line to toe: no trace to kick over and no compulsion to do anything. By consequence, a certain defect runs through everything . . . all slovenly, all out of plumb and untrue" (qtd. in Ricketts 197).

Then in 1896, a dispute between America and England over British Guiana flared up, and Kipling feared that the two powers would go to war. During that crisis, word was received that the German Kaiser had offered support to the Boers against the English in the Transvaal, and the combination events seemed to push Kipling "over the edge into outright hysteria" making him "so paranoid that for a time he convinced himself he was in serious personal danger" (Ricketts 218) . He felt as if he were "between two barrels like a pheasant," he wrote in a letter. "If the American mine is sprung it means dirt and slush and ultimately death either across the Canada border or in some disemboweled gunboat off Cape Hatteras. If the German dynamite is exploded equally it means slaughter and most probably on the high seas." An "inner eye" tells Kipling that he "shan't live to see it out: unless I bolt and hide myself in the wilds of Patagonia or the Pole. Even in that resort I should be dead or worse than dead" (qtd. in Carrington 178).

A few months later the final blow came, as Kipling quarreled with Carrie's brother, Beatty, a raucous but locally popular ne'er-do-well, even going so far as to have him arrested on assault charges. The scandal was seized upon by the newspapers, many of which took the opportunity to comment upon whether or not Kipling was liked by his neighbors and what sort of role he had played in local civic life. People took sides for or against the Kiplings; the privacy he had so cherished was shattered and paradise, once again, was lost.

In wartime conditions, Fairbairn wrote, "war neuroses" are experienced by those who are "haunted by bad objects against the return of which all defenses have broken down" (166). Here we see Kipling's defenses under attack, and a paralyzing depression setting in; Carrie reported that he slept all the time and was "dull, listless and weary" (Ricketts 224). By August of 1896, the family left for England. That Kipling has seen his life in Vermont as an imaginary return to the happiness of his Indian childhood seems clearly indicated by a comment made to visitors on the day before he left for England: "There are only two places in the world where I want to live – Bombay and Brattleboro. And I can't live in either" (Carrington 187).

The Kiplings returned to England in time for Victoria's Diamond Jubilee, an event, Denis Judd has written, which was used to "boost flagging national morale" and "divert attention from fundamental failures and chronic uncertainty." Through events like the Diamond Jubilee, Britain's "faltering great power status could . . . be underwritten by magnificent displays . . . and her position of global supremacy therefore preserved" (140). For the celebration, Kipling wrote "Recessional," a poem which contains a strikingly mixed message, noting British "dominion over palm and pine" but hinting at a scenario of collapse and even guilt, linking Britain to the sinful Biblical city of Nineveh. The poet implies that only sober caution and trust in God can protect the nation from catastrophe. The third stanza reads:

> Far-called, our navies melt away;
> On dune and headland sinks the fire:
> Lo, all our pomp of yesterday
> Is one with Nineveh and Tyre!
> Judge of the Nations, spare us yet,
> Lest we forget – lest we forget!   (*Gunga* 63)

The poem was unanimously applauded, and firmly established Kipling as a poet of empire. As Ricketts writes, both liberals and imperialists found much to like in the poem, though in letters Kipling insists he has not meant to question Britain's imperial role: "Any other breed of white man, with such a weapon to their hand, would have been captivating the round Earth in their own interests long ago" (qtd. in Ricketts 237). Despite Kipling's disclaimers however, there is a subtext of anxiety and guilt in the poem, making it a surprising piece with which to celebrate a moment of national triumph, suggesting that under that triumph lay a rich vein of national insecurity.

In the next few years, Kipling suffered a series of blows that replicated childhood trauma – the final loss of his American idyll and the death of a young daughter. At the same time Britain itself suffered a blow to its grandiose self image, the initial, humiliating defeats of the British by the tiny Boer republics. Against this background, Kipling's portrayal of empire shifted radically. No longer was empire seen as a place where young men passively suffer and accomplish little. Now, as shown by the short story, "A Sahib's War," empire was a place where sadistic punishment was to be inflicted upon degraded foes, with the survival of civilization itself at stake.

The Boer War, a fight to take control of the Boer Republics of Transvaal and The Orange Free State, which lay north of the English Cape Colony at the tip of southern Africa, was popularly seen as a crusade to protect the English-speaking population, which had flooded into the Transvaal upon the discovery of gold, from the rule of backward Afrikaners or Boers. Many asserted that southern Africa had to be united in English hands to maintain British standing in the world. Others, however, saw the conflict as representing "all that was reprehensible in British imperialism" fought against two weak and tiny republics on behalf of Cecil Rhodes, whose mining plans had not been supported by the leader of the Transvaal (Judd 155). But, if Kipling had earlier portrayed British Empire as a place where little of value was accomplished, and popular interest in empire as a "blind, brutal, British public's bestial thirst for blood" (*Light* 48), his position now seems completely reversed; he traveled to South Africa where he became intimate with Rhodes – who gave the Kiplings a home on one of his estates. Kipling put his newspaper skills to work turning out a propaganda sheet, writing much of the copy himself, including a stronger version of "The White Man's Burden," called "A Song of the White Men." With this poem, Kipling's portrayal of empire takes another step. Gone now is the sense of the futility of empire, but also gone is the notion, found in "White Man's Burden," that the British are sacrificing themselves for the good of the natives they rule. Replacing this is a hard, ruthless vision of a struggle for survival:

> Now, this is the faith that the White Men hold
> When they build their homes afar –
> Freedom for ourselves and freedom for our sons
> And, failing freedom, War.[3]

Kohut has described aggression in narcissistic individuals as exhibiting a "rage" which sets it off from other kinds of aggression. Often, Kohut argues, the narcissist was shamed or ridiculed as a child, and in adulthood wards off his continuing vulnerability to shame by attempting to shame others in a sort of preventive attack. In "sadistic re-enactments" of his own mistreatment, he attacks others in a spirit of revenge, even though these have not played a part in the original injury. Such misplaced rage, Kohut writes, is marked by its "utter disregard for reasonable limitations and a boundless wish to redress injury and to obtain revenge." (640).

This particular "flavor" of rage is on display in "A Sahib's War." The story is narrated by a Sikh fighter, who has come to southern Africa to serve his beloved master, a golden young English captain whom the Sikh adores like a son. Through this account of the love the colonized bear their British masters, Kipling suggests that the Boers have no good reason for fighting, but should love the English as does the Sikh. The Sikh is also used as a surrogate to display attitudes underlying the British role that may not be entirely seemly for the British themselves to express. The Sikh, for example, holds nakedly racist attitudes toward black Africans. And he also expresses a grandiose attitude toward empire, a vision of greatness that is dogged by a fear of collapse, and that echoes the underlying uncertainty of "Song of White Men." As the Sikh puts it, "Ye cannot in one place rule and in another bear service. Either ye must everywhere rule or everywhere obey" (Raine 208).

Finally, Kipling uses the Sikh to express a sadistic hatred for those who would challenge – and, as the Boers have done, temporarily defeat – the British, a hatred that is not consistent with the attitudes expected of those bearing the white man's burden, but which *is* consistent with the sadistic rage of the narcissist as described by Kohut, in which the narcissist is unable to see his enemy as "a center of independent initiative with whom he happens to be at cross-purposes" and thus a person, however wrong, something like himself ("Thoughts" 643).

In Kipling's story, the Boers are not seen as legitimate combatants or even as fully human, but as evil, bestial and deserving of the most sadistic treatment. When the British captain is killed by Boer farmers, the loyal Sikh goes to the farm for revenge. The Boers he finds there are shown to be profoundly degenerate, the mother is a "fat woman with the eyes of a swine and the jowl of a swine" and her son is an idiot, "a tall young man deprived of understanding. His head was hairless, no larger than an orange, and the pit of his nostrils was eaten away by a disease. He laughed and slavered and sported sportily" (Raine 214). Encountering these creatures, the Sikh enchains the woman whose "life and body" he claims. She pleads for mercy falling "upon her knees and lay along the ground, and pawed [his] boots and howled" (217). He is preparing to hang her son, taking care to position a lamp so that "she might see well," when a ghost of the dead captain appears to stop the proceedings, and the Sikh reluctantly turns the affair over to some British soldiers who arrive at this point.

Perhaps the intensity of the anger seen here is a result of the fact that Kipling, though he has written much about warfare, is actually close to the front for the first time, and witnessing the filth and disease that particularly marked the Boer conflict. Perhaps it is a result of the threat the English face, suffering their first serious reversals in recent memory at the hands of those whom they sought to colonize. Perhaps too it is due to the continued assaults upon Kipling's own self-esteem, the devouring nature of fame, as he seems to have experienced it, and the humiliation that resulted from his attempt to build a sanctuary in America. Certainly the sense of the vulnerability of young English men has always been present in Kipling's work, but the earlier stories do not display the desire to torture and humiliate one's enemies. Nor is there the fearful sense that all that is beloved, good and fine, is horribly vulnerable and can be wiped out in a moment. This, as Kohut has shown, is the inner world of the narcissist, a vacillation between grandiose fantasies of perfection, and an underside of loss, fear and rage. "A Sahib's War," with its desire for violent and sadistic revenge, strikes a new chord in that the enemies of the English are presented in such bestial terms, and that these desires are expressed so crudely, even if they are displaced onto a non-English proxy.

As the Boer War was still going on, Kipling published what would become his best-known and most popular novel, *Kim*. It is here, more than in any other work, that we see Kipling succumb completely to the grandiose fantasies that mark the victim of narcissistic disturbance. This fantasy is strikingly embodied in the person of Kim, the young English boy, orphaned in India. Though he is orphaned, he is by no means harmed – as the child Rudyard was so deeply harmed – by the disappearance of parents. Indeed Kim is the opposite of the miserable, helpless, friendless little boy that had been Rudyard Kipling from the ages of five to ten, for Kim is adored and respected by all. He has the omniscience of a god, knows everything about his environment, and his powers are acknowledged and praised by everyone around him. He knows none of the loss or sadness of the boy in "Baa Baa, Black Sheep" or of little Mohammed Din. While Mowgli was an outcast everywhere, Kim is at home everywhere, known as "Little Friend of All the World." He speaks several vernaculars, is savvy enough to understand all the shady schemes that are hatched in the bazaars, and at the same time has the spirituality to lead a holy man, a lama, on his quest for enlightenment. A beauty, he is beloved of women, but he – unlike Kipling's earlier young men in India – has no need for a mother or women in general and knows enough to avoid them. Plucky and tough, he is admired and respected, by the toughest of characters. In primary narcissistic heaven, Kim's perfection is mirrored by all around him.

But Kim's powers go beyond even this. Even as he owns native life, he simultaneously has a highly successful career as a British spy. This however does not present a problem. His love for the lama, whom he guides toward enlightenment, feels real, and one waits for Kim to come up against the contradiction that he is using the holy man's quest to escape the evil of the world as a cover from which to spy for the British. But Kim – all things to all people, native and British alike – never recognizes this as a contradiction. He is a full-fledged narcissist, able to use others without acknowledging or even recognizing what he is doing.

The only difficulty we ever see Kim face comes during a time of illness. Momentarily deprived of the energy that allows him to perform his perfection before mirroring others, Kim plunges into symptoms of depression to which the narcissist is prone. For the narcissist, Miller writes, "depression, the feeling of emptiness and self-alienation" come to the fore whenever "the drug of grandiosity fails, as soon as they are not 'on top,' not definitely the 'superstar' or whenever they suddenly get the feeling they failed to live up to some ideal image and measure they feel they must adhere to" (6). Weakened by illness, his powers momentarily failing him, Kim's "soul was out of gear with its surroundings – a cog wheel unconnected with any machinery." The noises around him "hit on dead ears." Kim's attempts to recover show the instantaneous shifting between grandiosity and emptiness that Kipling understands: "'I am Kim. I am Kim,' he repeats to himself. 'And what is Kim?' His soul repeated it again and again" (254). Within a few lines, however, the old Kim is back, and Kipling hurriedly causes the lama to sing his perfection: "'Never was such a *chela*. Temperate, kindly, wise, of ungrudging disposition, a merry heart upon the road, never forgetting, learned, truthful, courteous'" (255).

The evidence suggests that Kipling struggled for a time to find the truth of his experience, to express the sense of young men used and abused by those in power, an experience familiar to many boys and men of the era who had attended boarding school or gone into military or colonial service. With his venture to America, he tried to satisfy the yearning for some lost, good place, and in that safety to continue to probe his own experience. When that safety too was lost, and when the reality and the fantasy of British supremacy was challenged by the Boer War, Kipling retreated into grandiose dreams, taking, his immense popularity indicates, a good many of the shaken British public with him. With *Kim*, Kipling seems to have given up any real hope of recovering from his narcissistic wounds. No longer a commentator on hypocritical imperial power, he now embraces it completely, wrapping it in the gauze of impossible perfection. The helpless young Englishman seen in his earlier work, a boy struggling like a fly in the hypocritical webs of power has been transformed into a young English god, all seeing, all knowing, adored by all, and, strangely freed of the standard moral constraints.

6 ISAK DINESEN

A Passion for Africans

"To us, the man who adores the Negro is as 'sick' as the man who abominates him." FRANTZ FANON

In *Out of Africa*, Karen Blixen describes her farm in the "white highlands" of Kenya between 1913 and 1931 as an intoxicating world of air and light at six thousand feet. In this exhilarating setting, Blixen portrays herself as the benevolent and amused mistress of an immense coffee plantation, surrounded by adoring Africans with whom she lives in reciprocal harmony. In this book and in a second memoir, *Shadows on the Grass*, Blixen casts the Africans in a variety of roles. They are the loyal, if often comical, feudal retainers to her white queen. Paradoxically, they are also cast as attentive parents to her needy child, figures who are always there to pamper and admire her, and to love her unconditionally. And finally, as Blixen's life on the plantation lies in ruins, Africans are cast as nature's aristocrats, possessed of an inherent right to existence that eludes Blixen herself. In all of these scenarios, Blixen appears never to see the Africans as beings with lives of their own, separate from herself. Instead she uses them as screens upon which to project her own infantile yearning to be the omnipotent center of the world, her intense need for love and approval, and her desire for a sense of natural entitlement.

Blixen is not alone in her desire to create a romanticized vision of premodern simplicity and harmony far from industrialized, democratized Europe. By the 19th century, England was awash in nostalgia for medieval life, and the literature of imperialism frequently reveals the sense that forays into the rest of the world allow one to escape the conflicts of modernity and to return to a time when the lines separating ruler and ruled were more clearly defined. The desire to return to a past of great lords and devoted serfs seemed to represent an anxious response to the egalitarian ideas set into motion by Enlightenment rationalism, and to betray the fear that the rising tide of democracy would swamp European culture as the upper middle class had known it. Although neo-chivalric ideas of inherent nobility and right to rule may have been formulated to control new "internal barbarians," such ideas were also of great use, as Mark Girouard puts it, to those "bitten by the imperialist bug" (222). European imperialists, threatened by democracy and the attendant ills of socialism and trade unionism, could use conquered peoples to recreate a fantasy of the past, a time when methods of "ensuring subordination, obedience and loyalty" had not yet eroded (Hobsbawm 105).

If England's late 19th century reinvention of chivalry can be seen as the wish to return to a time before the "leveling" of rationalist ideas, it has also been seen as a kind of death wish, as the middle classes of Europe lost their "historic mission," and ideals of "peace, reason and progress" were replaced with those of "violence, instinct and explosion" (Hobsbawm 190). This recreation of chivalric attitudes comes to resemble a sort of group narcissism, fueled by cultural insecurity and a sense of displacement, alternating between domineering grandiosity and a sense of cataclysmic loss. These attitudes would result in a significant portion of Europe's youth "plung[ing] willingly, even enthusiastically, into the abyss" of World War I, Hobsbawm writes, "like people who had fallen in love" (190). A similar mood is reflected in Blixen's short stories, in which characters passionately desire greatness, dominance and acclaim, and are simultaneously propelled toward destruction.

The six thousand acres in Kenya over which Blixen reigned had been purchased for her by wealthy Danish relatives, and were worked by Africans who had been displaced by the arrival of the Europeans. The Africans survived by "squatting" on Blixen's vast acreage, and were required to pay for this privilege by working for her half the year. Though she was the beneficiary of cheap, stolen land and virtual slave labor, getting rich was not the chief aim of Blixen, who had come to Africa with her new husband, Baron Bror Blixen, a son of Swedish aristocrats. Neither Karen nor Bror were able to pay enough attention to the economics of the farm to make it pay, and it ultimately went bankrupt. Rather, Africa worked for both Karen and Bror as a magic kingdom in which each could play out infantile fantasy roles, Karen as lady of the manor, and Bror, who is said to have been the model for the guide in Ernest Hemingway's story "The Short Happy Life of Francis Macomber," as hard drinking, womanizing white hunter. For both, Africa offered the chance to live out the grandiose fantasies of the narcissist.

But narcissists, according to Heinz Kohut and others, are not born. Rather, they are created both by their families and their societies. In Blixen's case, the thwarted yearning for acceptance and approval, and the sustained, if masked assault upon self-esteem which marks the narcissist, is well documented in the author's early life. Karen Blixen – Tanne to her family – was the second of three girls born in rapid succession to Ingeborg

Westenholtz, daughter of a family of self-made millionaires, and Wilhelm Dinesen, son of a country family with connections to the greatest noblemen in Denmark. Wilhelm is described by Judith Thurman as a man in search of "a more intense experience of his being." An army officer in the Dano Prussian War, he later made a "traditional romantic pilgrimage" to North America where he sought "serenity in the wilderness, inspiration from the courage and simplicity of the natives"(13, 15). Although she was brought up among the powerful, puritanical, bourgeois women of her mother's family, Tanne still felt herself to be her father's favorite, defining herself "by opposition to the plebeians of her surroundings. She and her father made an aristocracy of two, and her greatest pride was that she was his and not 'theirs'" (Thurman 26).

When Wilhelm committed suicide in Karen's tenth year, however, this aristocracy was destroyed. The young girl's loss was intense and, Karen Blixen would come to feel later in life, crippling. With his death she was delivered back into the powerfully controlling arms of the Westenholzes. Among them the sense of a separate, special self, nurtured by her father would be repeatedly crushed, a ripe condition, as Kohut claims, for the creation of an adult ego that alternates between grandiose fantasies, and feelings of helplessness and inferiority. As Blixen's letters from Africa show, the Westenholzes, for all their intense closeness, viewed their children more as family assets than as separate individuals entitled to lives of their own. Blixen's letters to her "own beloved beloved wonderful little mother" are thick with phrases of love and longing and are endlessly apologetic about her own troubles and failures. But as affairs on the African farm worsen and as the family begins to pressure her, much against her will, to divorce the improvident Bror, Blixen also begins to express the sense that in losing her father she has lost the one person who was not bent upon changing her, controlling her or disciplining every impulse: "I think my greatest misfortune was Father's death," she writes in 1921. "Father understood me as I was, although I was so young, and loved me for myself ." The Westenholzes, on the other hand, "If they do care for me at all, do so in spite of my being as I am. They are always trying to change me into something quite different; they do not like the parts of me that I believe to be good" (Lasson 110). And Blixen reproaches herself bitterly for "the one great mistake" of accepting family financing for the African venture, declaring that if she manages to hold on in Africa it will be no thanks to the Westenholzes but rather "father who had done it for me. It is his blood and his mind that will bring me through" (110).

Blixen is hardly alone in using imperial opportunities to re-visit childhood conflict and loss. In his analysis of the private lives of key imperialists, Ronald Hyam shows that these figures frequently exhibit a high degree of immaturity, never outgrowing the fantasies and romantic ideals of childhood. Those at the forefront of imperial operations were often, Hyam writes, searching for stand-ins for missing or inadequate parents. And while Hyam acknowledges that the imperial enterprise is generally viewed as masculine, he notes that "the handful of women who contributed something notable to it seems also to confirm the thesis of emotional deprivation" (47).

Blixen, then, is not an uncommon imperialist in her desire to find in Africa a return to a thwarted, infantile perfection. In this search, Blixen would try to ally herself with those whom she believed embodied the aristocratic freedom, entitlement and reckless disdain of society's rules that she associated with her adventurer father. All of her life Karen would be drawn to aristocrats, becoming a hanger-on in the circle of her noble cousin Daisy Frijs, marrying Baron Bror Blixen after failing to attract his twin brother, Hans, allying herself with the English aristocrats in East Africa against the bourgeois settlers who disgusted her, falling in love with the son of a British lord, Denys Finch Hatton.

Not only did Blixen seek out aristocrats in real life, but much of her literary work, especially in the short story collection, *Seven Gothic Tales*, is also devoted to a tortured elaboration of the aristocratic personality as she envisions it. In these stories, written immediately after her return to Denmark and published three years before she wrote *Out of Africa*, Blixen repeatedly portrays characters which demonstrate both sides of the narcissistic coin, grandiose desires for freedom, power and adoration, which are only briefly sustained before a plunge into loss, emptiness and death. Blixen's *Tales* cast a light on the imperial psyche, as her characters are often tortured by the sense that they are created by the gaze of others, even as they struggle, in their turn, to create others. One such figure, the charlatan Kasparson in the story "The Deluge at Norderney," succinctly expresses both a grandiose sense of omnipotence alternating with a nagging fear of falseness and emptiness. "Nothing in the world have I ever loved, except [the peasants]," Kasparson says. "If they would have made me their master I would have served them all my life. If they would only have fallen down and worshipped me, I would have died for them. But they would not" (76).

This expression of desire gives us a psychological context out of which to read the glowing portrait of Blixen's relationship with Africans as these fantasies contain the tortured sense that the attempt to live in freedom and disdain for convention will always be engulfed by cataclysm. Even those who appear to exhibit the wild disregard for convention that only aristocrats, in Blixen's view, can maintain, often must do so in a masquerade. In what amounts to a portrait of the divided self of narcissistic disorder, with its oscillations between grandiosity and tortured emptiness, these figures, when faced with the powerful constraints of society, can only be their wild, free selves when masked. The desire for the freedom to be one's authentic self has been perverted into the need to play a part, and in accepting their roles, the characters seem to acknowledge their inner emptiness.

"The Deluge at Norderney," for example, in which one nearly fantastic story opens into the next in the manner of *Arabian Nights*, features several characters of noble blood who attempt to escape intensely controlling backgrounds in which a separate and authentic sense of self has not been allowed to develop. The central figure, Miss Malen Nat-og-Dag, is the last member of an old aristocratic family. Despite her noble blood, she was brought up in a repressive environment reminiscent of that created by the puritanical Westenholzes, where she was taught to value chastity above all else (17). As a result, her sexual life has been limited to sinful fantasy. In slightly mad old age, and thanks to the "wildness" of her aristocratic blood, she has come to believe that her fantasies were real and that she actually has lived a life of sexual debauchery. This sort of fantasy, she argues, is noble and even godlike as it frees one from the pettiness of reality: "Truth is for tailors and shoemakers," she remarks. "I on the contrary have always held that the Lord had a penchant for masquerades . . . the Lord himself. . . seems to me to have been masquerading pretty freely" when he came to earth (24). Here Blixen paints freedom and "wildness" as, ultimately, an act, since her protagonist has actually lived the chaste life she was taught to revere, only pretending to have escaped its repressive hold. For Blixen, however, this pretense is heroic, and at the end of the story the old woman is likened to Scheherazade, spinning fantasies to keep death at bay, even though, in the end, death wins.

Another character in "The Deluge at Norderney," the young countess Calypso von Platen Hallermund, is shown struggling and ultimately failing to escape a background in which the authentic self is brutally suppressed. Calypso is brought up by an uncle who detests women, preferring the company of young boys. In this he is reminiscent of Wilhelm Dinesen and his passionate love for his soldiers when he was an officer in the Danish and French armies. This was a love, Wilhelm wrote in a letter, which was similar to the love of women, except that it was not limited to one person. His daughter would later compare her father's love for his men to her passion for her African servants. "It was the same thing," she writes, "with the Natives and me" (*Out* 19).

The uncle in "Deluge" tries to solve the problem of Calypso's gender by dressing her and treating her like a boy. But when it became clear she was a girl, he "turned his eyes away from her forever and annihilated her . . . Her girl's beauty was her sentence of death . . . Since then she has not existed" (44). If the uncle resembles Wilhelm, Calypso resembles Karen, who felt herself as a small girl to have been created as someone different from her sisters by the companionship of her father. Wilhelm Dinesen's suicide occurred when his daughter was ten, the age at which girls usually exhibit the first visible signs of puberty, and the young

Tanne may have believed, as does Calypso, that her impending woman-
hood was in some way connected to her abandonment. Calypso feels
that, no longer boyish, she does not exist "for nobody ever looked at
her" (45). And, as Karen Blixen sought relationships with profoundly
unreliable men who bore a resemblance to her aristocratic father – the
uninterested Hans Blixen, the reckless Bror Blixen, and the elusive Denys
Finch Hatton – so Calypso is drawn to the suits of armor that stand in
the castle corridors. These "looked like real men," and she feels they
would have supported her "had they not all been hollow" (45). In the
sad world that Blixen portrays in these stories, not only is one denied
one's authentic self, but those who might come to one's aid are themselves only attractive masks.

Two other figures should be noted from "The Deluge at Nordernay,"
both of whom struggle to transcend identities thrust upon them. Jonathan,
the bastard son of a great nobleman, is acknowledged in adulthood by his
father, who declares that the son will inherit his riches and his name if the
father can see his own "soul . . . showing itself" in the young man.
Suddenly the eyes of the fashionable world are on the young man who
abhors his new situation. Now his every attitude, including his sadness
and his contempt for his father's offerings, are taken as representations of
the "soul" of his father (33). As such, they become fashion statements to
be imitated by all the elegant young men of Copenhagen, and lovely
women beg to join him if he decides upon suicide. There is absolutely
nothing he can do, Blixen shows, to escape the controlling, creating hand
of the parent.

Finally, perhaps the greatest effort at transcendence of all is made by
a man introduced as the aristocratic Cardinal von Sehestedt, son of "an
old and noble race," a man of such stature that people believed he could
work miracles, even walk on water. When the dikes break in Nordernay,
the cardinal is among the rescuers who boat out into the flood to take
survivors to safe ground. He, along with Miss Nat-og-Dag, the Countess
Calypso, and Jonathan are moved by the nobility of their blood to give
their places in the rescue boat to a family of peasants, and they remain
behind in the hayloft of a barn that could give way to the flood at any
moment. The cardinal, who opines that all artists, kings and gods have a
bit of "charlatanry" in them, reveals at the end of an evening of story-
telling that he is not actually the cardinal at all, but rather the cardinal's
valet, Kasparson, the bastard son of a French duke. Kasparson has
murdered the cardinal and assumed his identity. With no standing of his
own as a bastard, he has been forced to take refuge in a wide variety of
disguises and has become a connoisseur of appropriated roles. Of these,
his favorite was that of the heroic, miracle-working cardinal, adored of
the common people.

In the end, all of these desperate figures come together in the precarious loft as the flood waters rise, all expressing both the desire to be free of roles thrust upon them, as well as the sense that there is finally no inner authenticity to be found, that the self must constantly be created and nourished through playacting, and the homage of others. At the close of the evening the hayloft is engulfed; the four have fled convention, but their escape has ended in annihilation.

In a short story called "The Dreamers," one can see not only Blixen's sense of what her life must become after returning to Denmark from Africa, but also a portrayal, striking in its grandiosity, of how Blixen viewed herself in relation to her humble but admiring "public," the Africans on her farm. The story is the first Blixen wrote after the loss of the African farm and her return to her mother's house in Denmark, and, as she acknowledged to her friend Thorkild Bjornvig, the protagonist was modeled upon herself (Bjornvig 211). At first Blixen's protagonist, a young woman, named Pellegrina, seems to have achieved the transcendence so desired by the characters in "The Deluge at Norderney." A fabulous opera singer, Pellegrina makes her hearers understand "the meaning of heaven and earth, of the stars, life and death, and eternity," and for her greatness she is adored by her public (331).

Pellegrina has two great passions in her life. One passion is for herself as a great soprano, a love compared to the love that a priest has for the image of the Virgin. In this passion, she is fierce and jealous, furious that she cannot sing all the parts on stage at once. The other passion is for her audience, especially the poor people who sit in the galleries, and even her desire for the applause of the connoisseurs is for the sake of the poor people. When she sang, she muses, they "stamped . . . shrieked, and wept over her" and she "loved them beyond everything in the world." Her love for the poor people was "mighty," but at the same time "as gentle as the love of God." She grieved for them, gave them money, "even sold her clothes for them." They for their part knew she was giving them her all and "never begged much" (334). Pellegrina has love affairs, but they are disappointing; the real world is a shabby place compared with the brilliant dramas of the stage – compared, that is, to her own fantasies. Her one satisfying relationship is with an adoring and wealthy father figure, who devotes his life to her service, and to whom she turns "as a child to its mother" (332).

Then, in a horrible fire that destroys the magical world of the stage with its cardboard houses and streets, Pellegrina is badly injured, so that her voice is irreparably damaged. This destruction, Blixen told Bjornvig represents her own loss of the farm and Africa. So immense is Pellegrina's loss that it seems she herself has been burned up, left "immovable, black and charred" (339). She grieves not only for her lost grandeur but especially for the poor people who are bereft of her presence. For them, she believes, she has been the one shining light in an otherwise bleak existence: "Their one star had fallen; they were left in the dark of the night – the galleries which had laughed and wept with her" (341).

Pellegrina's response to this loss is striking. So bound up is her sense of herself with the grandeur of her role as diva, and with the adoration of her "poor people," that she does not even try to maintain a stable sense of identity without these attributes. Although she continues to live – like Karen Blixen she survives a suicide attempt – she determines that she will "not be one person again . . . I will always be many persons from now. Never again will I have my heart and my whole life bound up with one woman, to suffer so much" (345). She feels that in this decision she has finally discovered the secret to human happiness: "Is it not strange that no philosopher has thought of this, and that I should hit upon it?" (346).[1] But splitting oneself into a number of identities does not bring her happiness, only inevitable fiery destruction. In her various guises – as a prostitute, a revolutionary, and a saintly and rich young woman – Pellegrina wins the passionate love of men, but always runs away at the height of their devotion, leaving, it seems, before she can be left. Sadly, even a self that is consciously false is still vulnerable to destruction. Pursued by her admirers, Pellegrina is finally apprehended in a mountain pass. In one final gesture, she unites the desire for transcendence with the certainty of doom. Seeing that her pursuers were upon her she "spread out her wings and flew away," but her flight is really a plunge into an abyss, and she falls to her death (327).

In these stories, begun in Africa and completed in Denmark after the loss of the African farm, we see the yearning to transcend the strictures of an upbringing in which one is required to mirror others' needs. We see too the desire to achieve wild-hearted greatness, and to be worshipped by those who could never approach or challenge one's own glory. Blixen's characters, most of whom are emboldened to rebel against their lot by virtue of a touch of noble blood, usually can be traced to the author herself. Either they have not been allowed to form an authentic self, or their sense of self is so disastrously intertwined with the attitudes of others, so precariously alternating between narcissistic grandiosity and loss, that it is permanently at risk of destruction. So harrowing is this existence that one must escape into disguise, and through her character, Pellegrina, Blixen tries to imagine giving up entirely the attempt to form a coherent self. In both "Deluge" and "Dreamers" the struggle to find a place where the self can rest, even temporarily, ends in violent death.

The tortured grandiosity of these stories, with their fantasies of dominance, adoration and annihilation prepares us to understand the psychological underpinnings of Blixen's portrait of her life in Africa and to consider the complex way in which at least one European imperialist makes use of Africans who have been made dependent upon her. First, we must consider the most obvious use, Africans as feudal retainers to

Blixen's great lady. In Africa, Blixen writes, "everything you saw made for greatness and freedom" (*Out* 4), and it is the perfect stage for Blixen to play her grand role. As props, Blixen acquires Scottish deerhounds, animals which she believes impart a "feudal atmosphere" (72). She dresses her servants in livery and has them stand behind her at the table. Her home is portrayed as a feudal court where she and her aristocratic friends, in contrast to the cautious bourgeois settlers, hunt, tell heroic stories and "risk [their] lives unnecessarily" in pursuit of glory and excitement (242). Blixen sometimes laments the hard lot of the natives, but such comments are almost always made as criticisms of the lower class of settlers who lack the quality of *noblesse oblige* and do not understand the reciprocal bond between master and servant. It is through this bond, Blixen believes, that identity is discovered. As the master's sense of power and dominance is reflected in the servant, so the servant is created by his devotion. The servant, she writes, "needs a master in order to know himself" (*Shadows* 409). In her understanding and love for the natives, Blixen allies herself with Denys Finch Hatton and the other English aristocrats of East Africa. One sign of these relationships is the affectionate nickname, and Blixen, who is known as Baroness Blixen, reports herself to have been given the name, "Lioness Blixen" by some of her servants.[2]

Blixen shows herself as performing a variety of paternalistic roles, acting as judge to the people on her farm, taking it as her role to keep the peace, though she knows nothing of their law. Like a medieval king, she recognizes the need occasionally to humble her nobles, walking out on the elders who seem to ignore her in a legal assembly and enjoying their subsequent dismay: "They then stumbled on to their old legs in great haste, and began to flap their arms at me. I waved my hand to them in return, and rode off" (102). In addition to serving as judge, she doctors the people, and teaches them, though her instruction is limited to culinary arts and other aspects of service.

The reciprocal relationship is further portrayed when Blixen must sell the farm. The Africans are shown to be nearly disbelieving that she could actually be leaving, and desperately dependent upon her to settle their future. In this Blixen attributes to the natives a grasp of the medieval European notion that the noble lord holds his position by divine right, that he is a kind of lesser god. Writing about the Africans' response to her loss of the farm, she reports that they see it as a sort of "act of God" for "in some respects . . . the white men fill in the mind of the Natives the place that is, in the mind of the white men, filled by the idea of God" (386).[3]

The role that Blixen intends to create for herself is that of feudal master. But there are times in these studiedly self-mythologizing memoirs, when the mask slips, and we are allowed to glimpse Blixen as the lost child, standing not as lord to the Africans, but as a child with the Africans cast in the role of parents. She relies on them for patient and consistent support and affection, needing them to believe in her goodness, as her own family – at least since her father's death – has not done.

In *Out of Africa*, Blixen shows the Africans as providing a kind of loving background to her life. With them she becomes a well-tended infant encircled by an adoring world that is focused entirely on her, allowing her to float in a sea of primary narcissism bliss. "From my first weeks in Africa," Blixen writes, "I had felt a great affection for the Natives. . . . The discovery of the dark races was to me a magnificent enlargement of my world . . . if someone with an ear for music had happened to hear music for the first time when he was already grown up; their cases might have been similar to mine. After I had met with the Natives, I set out the routine of my daily life to the Orchestra" (*Out* 18).

The love that Blixen feels for the Africans is shown to be reciprocated in both *Out of Africa* and *Shadows on the Grass*, and she portrays herself, as Robert Langbaum wrote in an early study of her work, "surrounded by a circle of adoration" (40). Throughout the book, her "boys," as she calls the men who work the farm, are shown in the role of doting parents, taking an interest in all of her affairs, from her attempt to write a book to her wearing apparel to her finances. And the Africans are shown displaying a tender concern for their mistress's feelings. In garnering this affection, Blixen portrays herself as unusual in her relationship with Africans. Like a favored child, she alone is the apple of their eye. Late in life, she would tell a magazine interviewer: "I am the only white person the Natives really loved" (Thurman 437).

The most intimate surrogate parenting is performed by the servant Farah, a Somali man about her age who would attend her throughout her stay in Kenya, and for whom she cares, she writes in a letter home, "almost as much as anyone in the world" (Lasson 124). Like a firm but loving parent, Farah is always there, and in the section devoted to him in *Shadows on the Grass*, he is shown to believe in and support her own vision of herself as a great-hearted noble. As her chief servant, he demands that her house be "run in a grand style," insisting that she offer champagne when the importance of the guests calls for it, scouring Nairobi to find an ingredient for a special dish to be served a visiting prince (*Shadows* 420–21).

Blixen was not able to depend upon her husband, Bror, to play an adult role in financial matters; at the time of their divorce he was "wanted by the police" and "hiding out in the Masai Reserve without a tent or shoes" (Lasson 124). Her family, of course, supported her financially, but over the years they made it increasingly clear that the money was to be used to further their aims of profit, not her desire to build a grand life for herself in Africa; finally their support was withdrawn. Her lover, Denys Finch Hatton, remembered by those who knew him as more inclined toward love affairs with boys than with women (Boyles 24), was in any case clearly commitment phobic. But in Farah, as he is drawn in *Shadows on the Grass*, she has someone she can rely upon. He manages her financial affairs properly, and is shown to be even more concerned about her dignity and well-being than she is herself. On one occasion he declines to give her money she has asked for to buy a new pair of slacks, as he believes the money should be saved for an item essential to her image, riding boots sent from England: "Farah had good knowledge of riding-boots and felt it to be below my dignity to walk about in boots made by the Indians of Nairobi" (421). When Blixen receives a new evening dress from France, and is modeling it for the other servants who are full of admiration, Farah, like a careful parent, decides when enough praise is enough. He watches the proceedings "not insensitive to popularity," "approving" but "stern" and at the right moment brings out the bowl of tobacco that signals the end of the session. Portraying herself as basking childishly in the praise, Blixen asks him to let her hear a little more, but he responds firmly, "No, Memsahib, no. Now these Kikuyus have said enough about this frock. Now it is time that they have this tobacco" (435).

One of the most joyous times in Blixen's African idyll comes during World War I when she goes on a three-month safari alone with male African servants. Here there is delicious danger of lions and other animals, but she is safe among her men, and in the evenings they entertain her with stories, "strange happenings in Somaliland, or tales out of the Koran, and the Arabian Nights" (279). Here too, the servants stand in as good parents, unconditional in their affection and tender in their care: "My people showed great forbearance with my ignorance of oxen, harness and Safari ways; they were indeed as keen to cover it up as I was myself." The men pamper her as if she were a delicate child: "They carried bath-water for me on their heads a long way across the plain, and when we outspanned at noon, they constructed a canopy against the sun, made out of spears and blankets for me to rest under" (281–82). Cared for like a precious infant, Blixen seems to regress to a state of primary narcissism, in which she and the world are blissfully one: "How beautiful were the evenings of the Masai Reserve when after sunset we arrived at the river or the water-hole . . . The air was cold to the lungs, the long grass dripping wet, and the herbs on it gave out their spiced astringent scent. In a little while on all sides the Cicada would begin to sing. The grass was me, and the air, the distant invisible mountains were me, the tired oxen were me. I breathed with the slight night-wind in the thorn trees" (283–84).

Indeed, Blixen often ascribes to the natives the magical all-seeingness that small children assume of their parents, and she sees them as existing to reflect her own desires back to her, indeed as *teaching* her the nature of her own desires through this reflection: "They knew me through and through and were conscious of decisions I was going to take before I was certain of them myself" (20). Here the natives are portrayed as functioning in a way that is similar to that of D. W. Winnicott's attentive mother, who, in her responsiveness to her baby's physical and emotional needs, allows the child to learn and value its own subjectivity (17). Blixen's Danish family has placed many demands upon her, but in Africa, the focus is entirely upon her own, still infantile needs. And as the infant sees the parent as a part of herself, Blixen sees that upon coming to know Africans a "unity" has been created in her life, that of master and servant, as for each, "the play of colours would fade and his timbre abate were he to stand alone" (*Shadows* 409).

Blixen describes this love most urgently when writing about her fight to keep the farm after her relatives finally refuse to continue underwriting its losses. For several years she struggled alone to hold onto the farm, and in letters home she describes the land as her "child," the "only one I have in this life" (Lasson 131). The farm is all that makes her who she is she cries in these frantic letters, and without it she feels she will die (314). But bankruptcy looms and the family withdraws its support. In this crisis, depressed, ill and sleepless, Blixen feels she has no one to rely on except the loyal Africans. As she is being forced off the farm she compares herself to Napoleon retreating from Moscow, and her "squatters," who will also be evicted, to his soldiers. While it is generally thought that Napoleon "went through agonies" at seeing his army "suffering and dying" around him, Blixen writes, she feels that "he would have dropped down dead on the spot if he had not had them. In the night, I counted the hours till the time when the Kikuyus should turn up again by the house" (*Out* 344).

Finally, if Blixen portrays the Africans as serfs to her lord, and simultaneously as parents to her infant, she also sees in the Africans a kind of natural aristocracy for which she has yearned all of her life. Blixen's constant likening of the Africans to animals, particularly domestic animals, undoubtedly has a dehumanizing effect as Kenyan writer, Ngugi wa Thiong'o, charged (*Barrel* 56). But the comparison of Africans to wild animals also, contradictorily, reflects Blixen's envy of a natural entitlement she feels they possess, a sense of rightness in nature that cannot be undone by society's criticisms or demands. Blixen's views of animals, as she explained to Thorkild Bjornvig, is of creatures which "conform exactly to God's ideas and become what he means them to be. They do not interfere with God's plan as humans do" (202). The wild animal, then, is like the aristocrat, who is granted his place by God, and who need not clamber and strive like the bourgeois businessmen of the Westenholz family. Natural aristocrats may roam freely without cares or responsibilities as did Wilhelm Dinesen, Bror Blixen and Denys Finch Hatton. They do not have to worry about who and what they are; they just are: "When a creature on this earth is fulfilling God's plan," Bjornvig writes in

Karen Blixen – the Danish author who took the pen name Isak Dinesen – on safari in Kenya in 1914. With European men away for the duration of World War I, Blixen went on a three-month safari alone with male African servants. The men, Blixen wrote later, pampered her as if she were a delicate child: "They carried bath-water for me on their heads a long way across the plain, and when we outspanned at noon, they constructed a canopy against the sun, made out of spears and blankets for me to rest under."

describing Blixen's view, "identity is no problem. [Humans] can use the wild animal in its integrity as an example" (203). This understanding of the wild animal parallels Blixen's understanding of Africans. Her servant Farah was, as she says in *Shadow on the Grass*, a "wild animal" and as such, "nothing in the world would ever stand between him and God" (*Shadows* 418).

This sense that the African has a place in nature that the European in general, and Blixen in particular, can never attain, may also help us understand Blixen's account of the death of the man Kitosch. The death follows a beating given to Kitosch by his master for riding a horse home when he had been told to walk it. Blixen, however, attributes the death to the man's own will to die. This incident appears to occur at a time when Blixen herself feels figuratively beaten and abused by her financial backers who are forcing her to sell the farm and to give up her African existence. Indeed, in a letter concerning Blixen's protests over giving up the farm, her powerful aunt describes her as a horse that needs the whip; meanwhile, as the financial crisis closes in, Blixen repeatedly hints of suicide, making one failed attempt. In this context, we can read that Blixen has drawn Kitosch as achieving what she herself failed to achieve. In causing his own death through his wish to die, as Blixen claims he does, he escapes the "humiliation" of being thrown "out of existence" by Europeans (*Out* 294), a humiliation that Blixen, who is being thrown out of her African existence by her Danish backers, does not escape. Blixen allows herself to be controlled, and returns meekly, like a tamed animal to her family home, but Kitosch, as she imagines him, cannot be so controlled: "This strong sense in him of what is right and decorous . . . with his firm will to die . . . stands out with a beauty of its own. In it is embodied the fugitiveness of the wild things who are, in the hour of need, conscious of a refuge somewhere in existence; who go when they like; of whom we can never get hold" (294).

Blixen's description of Kitosch willing his own death, rather than submitting to others is reminiscent of a similar well-known fantasy found in Henrik Ibsen's 1890 play *Hedda Gabler*. Here, the title character clings to the belief that the unconventional Eilert Lovborg has committed suicide in a last great act "that shimmers with spontaneous beauty," that he has had "the courage to live life after his own mind." Hedda clings to this belief, even though it becomes apparent that Lovborg has actually been shot in the stomach during a fight (298). As Ngugi has suggested, Blixen's portrayal of Kitosch has everything to do with European attitudes and desires, and nothing to do with the lives of Africans, as it "ascribed to Kitosch the aesthetic pose of transcendence, ignoring the political and human consequences of the beating" (qtd. in Pelensky *Life* 97). Such a portrayal demonstrates Blixen's failure to grasp both the horror of a man being brutally beaten to death for a petty infraction of his master's orders;

as well as her own complicity in the death. Here as elsewhere, the Africans are not really themselves; rather, they function as a screen upon which Blixen, like Hedda Gabler, projects her own intense need to believe in transcendent escape.

It is striking that so many who have written about Blixen have accepted without question her portrayal of loving reciprocity between herself and the Africans, and her sense that her presence is beneficial to them. Blixen's self-portrayal as the loving and beloved mistress of the Africans on her farm was generally taken for fact when her book was published, according to her biographer Judith Thurman, and continues to be accepted, as evidenced by the glowing film version of *Out of Africa* made in 1985. Abdul R. JanMohamed, who writes frequently about colonial relationships, sees Blixen as a "major exception to the . . . pattern of conquest and irresponsible exploitation," noting her "largess toward her squatters" that he finds "not consciously or deliberately humane" but "based on an implicit trust and affection. She has genuine respect for all her servants, particularly for their pride" (147).

Yet not everyone believes Blixen's account of the love she and the Africans shared. Ngugi has expressed outrage that Blixen could be "canonized" for her portrayal of Africans as "dogs, hyenas, jackals and the like" (63). And Olga Anastasia Pelensky, another Blixen biographer, further complicates the picture of a loving relationship between Blixen and the Africans who worked on her farm by noting that in unpublished papers Blixen lists the people on her farm as "slaves" and herself as "owner" and that Blixen caused a stir by an interview with *Life* magazine when she said "she wouldn't mind owning slaves." The wish was "fanciful," Pelensky explains, as Blixen was "thinking of the slavery in the *Arabian Nights*, a glamorous and exotic phenomenon" (Pelensky *Life* 95).

Despite her passion for the Africans, Blixen's work lacks any acknowledgment of what her "boys" have lost as a result of her presence. When Blixen's farm was sold, her squatters too were forced to leave. Here for the first time, Blixen appears to recognize what it must be for them to lose their ancestral land. She puts their case feelingly: "It is more than their land that you take away from the people, whose Native land you take. It is their past as well, their roots and their identity." They face, she writes, "the shame of extinction" (*Out* 387,388). Despite this understanding, Blixen never takes the next step, never recognizes that Europeans like herself have been responsible for driving millions of people from the land that has contained their past, roots and identity, not just for a period of seventeen years but for generations past and to come. Instead, the Africans' identification with the land seems to date only from her arrival on the farm; it is only as "her people," as residents of her domain that their loss can be recognized. Finally, one suspects that Blixen, who feels she can't survive without the farm, is writing so feelingly not of the Africans' "extinction" but of her own.

Perhaps it is in this light that we may best view Blixen's writing on Africa. Her great work, *Out of Africa*, was written after she had returned to live out her life in her mother's house in Denmark. She had been utterly defeated in her bid to escape the control of her family and their narrow bourgeois existence, and had been forced to acknowledge that even her years of apparent escape were in fact allowed and controlled by her family from the beginning. Looking back, she writes Africa as a doomed dream of power and brilliance, with the Africans playing a cast of fantasy figures, the loyal serfs, the adoring parents, the natural aristocrats who dare what she does not dare. She does not grasp what has been done to Africans – what she herself has done to them – because her entire attention is taken up, obsessively, with what has been done to herself.

AFTERWORD
WTC, SEPTEMBER 11; INDIAN
"MUTINY," 1857

Two Studies in the Psychology of Embattled Superpower

"The psychoanalyst must not shrink from the task of applying his knowledge about the individual to the field of history, particularly to the crucial role of human aggression as it has shaped the history of man. . . . We will reach tangible results by focusing our attention on human aggression as it arises out of the matrix of archaic narcissism, i.e. on the phenomenon of narcissistic rage." HEINZ KOHUT

The September 11, 2001, attacks on America and their aftermath hold many striking similarities to another set of attacks that took place almost a hundred and fifty years earlier, when, in 1857, British rule in India was seriously challenged for the first time. That event, which has been called the "Indian Mutiny," was an uprising of native soldiers, aided by peasants and other groups. Although the two situations would not, on the surface, appear to have much in common, they are similar in many ways. In both cases, the attackers claimed to be defending their religion from Western affront. In both, those masterminding the attacks had concluded that the superpower they opposed was secretly weak and corrupt, and easy to topple. In both cases the attacks were directly aimed at civilians whose loss of life was spectacular in its horror. In both, the countries attacked were stunned and bewildered by the ferocity of hatred that could prompt such acts; many concluded that only pure "evil" – and in particular the evil of one individual mastermind – could be responsible. In both cases the attacks were followed by fervent self-mythologizing, as Britain and America alike indulged in patriotic displays that extolled their own virtuous qualities. In both cases the retaliation was massive and furious, and despite great initial popular support, fear was eventually expressed that the responses were excessive, irrational and even sadistic.

These similarities prompt a closer consideration of the "Mutiny" and Britain's actions in the aftermath of the Indian rebellion, as a way of

☆ 115 ☆

gaining perspective on America's position, attitudes and actions at home and in the world after September 11th.

The nature and magnitude of the British retaliation suggests that the country was reacting to more than physical attack. Rather, the response suggests that what had also been attacked was a shared sense of narcissistic grandiosity. When such grandiosity is threatened, according to Heinz Kohut, the "rage" that results has a particular flavor. While it is appropriate to engage in the "mature aggression" of those rationally fighting a dangerous external foe, there is another form of aggression, an irrational rage against what is felt to be a "flaw in a narcissistically perceived reality" ("Thoughts" 644). This type of aggression, Kohut asserts, is marked by the need to "undo the hurt by whatever means," and by a "compulsion" in the pursuit of revenge which "gives no rest to those who have suffered a narcissistic injury" (638). Not only individuals but whole groups, Kohut writes, may be drawn in to the "unrestrained pursuit of grandiose aims" as exemplified by "the ruthlessly pursued ambitions of Nazi Germany and of the German population's total surrender to the will of the Fuhrer" (620).

Such an irrational rage can be detected in the retaliatory British atrocities in India, as well as in a changed attitude toward Indians, including calls for genocide. A similar "compulsion" to revenge backed by the ultimate might of 21st century America is a terrifying prospect. This prompts the question: Has America responded to September 11 as a narcissistic injury, an assault upon a cherished self-image of benevolent, democratic goodness? Or have Americans managed to respond to a real attack with realistic, appropriate "mature aggression"?

The question of whether these two superpowers were and are responding, at least in part, to the sense that what was attacked was a grandiose self-image is a tantalizing one. In both cases those credited with masterminding the attacks claimed that the superpowers were just that: grandiose "paper tigers" whose self-proclaimed goodness and power was a sham. While it was a disaffected Hindu prince, Nana Sahib who was widely seen as the main villain of the "Mutiny" for allowing the murder of women and children, the idea for an uprising is believed, according to Andrew Ward, to have first occurred to his young Muslim adviser, who conceived the notion that the British were not the indomitable power they seemed.

The adviser, Azimulla Khan, an English speaker, had visited England on a mission to intercede with the government on Nana Sahib's behalf in a dispute regarding the prince's estate. There the image of imperial Britain that had been cultivated in India, that of a magically rich, powerful, and beautiful land with fine liberal traditions and a queen like a goddess, rapidly came undone. The famous English countryside appeared "harsh and forbidding," to Azimullah, while "industrial

An illustration from *History of the Indian Mutiny: Giving Detailed Account of the Sepoy Insurrection in India*, published in 1859 and depicting the massacre of English officers and their wives at Jhansi. The depiction of half-clothed women suggests one of the often repeated themes of "mutiny" literature, that the reason for rebelling against England could be found in the inherent "evil" of Indian sexual appetites. Though there was no evidence that sexual assaults occurred, it was obsessively suggested in the voluminous literature devoted to the "mutiny" that the rape of English women – accompanied by "unspeakable tortures" – was a central aim of the rebels.

smoke and waste and the frigid, incessant rain made the slums of London worse than anything India's cities had to offer" (Ward 47). Azimullah saw the storied English queen, "a squat little woman in the sway of her German husband," and read "fretful editorials" which made Britain "seem less the monolithic giant . . . and more a divided and depleted nation." Meanwhile, British troops had been chased out of Afghanistan, and English soldiers in the Crimea were sick and starving amid reports of negligence and incompetence among the officers. It was no wonder, Andrew Ward writes, that Azimulla "began to brood on what had once seemed too outlandish a notion to consider seriously: the expulsion of the British from India" (46–47).

Similarly, the man credited with masterminding the September 11 attacks, Osama bin Laden, in an interview with *Esquire* magazine in 1999, tells of how the Muslim mind has been "cleared" of the "myth of superpowers" (Miller, John). In the interview, bin Laden explains the process by which this "myth" was expelled. First, the mighty Soviet Union was defeated in its 1979 invasion of Afghanistan by Muslim fighters so that "with Allah's help their flag was folded a few years later and thrown in the trash and there was nothing left to call the Soviet Union." The lesson here, bin Laden indicates, was that committed fighters could defeat one of the mightiest powers on earth. Next, bin Laden saw his own soldiers shoot down American helicopters who were engaged in a UN-sanctioned rescue mission in Somalia. The world saw the body of a naked American soldier dragged through the streets, after which America hastily withdrew. "The youth were surprised at the low morale of the American soldiers," bin Laden says in the interview, "and realized more than before that the American soldier was a paper tiger and after a few blows ran in defeat. And America forgot all . . . about being the world leader . . . and left, dragging their corpses and their shameful defeat."

Not only American power, but also notions of America as a force for freedom or humanity in the world are portrayed as hollow. The claim that the American mission in Somalia was to save starving people is rejected: "Why should we believe that was the true reason America was there?" bin Laden asks. "Everywhere else they went where Muslims lived, all they did was kill children and occupy Muslim land." And bin Laden claims that America habitually commits this lowest of all acts, harming and killing children, both in Palestine and in Iraq where "American-led sanctions resulted in the death of one million Iraqi children."

If men like Azimulla Khan and Osama bin Laden claim that the great powers are hollow at heart, what response was provoked? Did the superpowers respond with "rational aggression"? Or do we see them reacting with enraged panic to the suggestion that they are weak and hollow, their power and their famed superiority easily punctured by determined bands of true believers?

Workmen in New York City on the first anniversary of the September 11, 2001 terrorist attacks. After 9/11, the American flag was on display everywhere in the New York City area. In lower Manhattan, site of the World Trade Center attack, immense flags covered the windows on upper floors of office buildings. A New York City newspaper published a full-paged flag designed to be cut out and displayed, and it could be seen for months afterward in many store windows. In the surrounding suburbs, flags flew from virtually every front porch. Many cars bore flag bumper stickers and it was even possible to buy plastic flags fitted with a suction device which allowed them to be mounted and flown from the outside of a car.

In the Indian case, the uprising was triggered by the court martial and subsequent public humiliation of Indian soldiers in the service of the East India Company who refused to use a new variety of greased cartridge issued by the British. The cartridges, which were coated with both pig and cow fat, and which had to be torn open, or, in the heat of battle, more likely bitten off, managed to outrage the religious sensibilities of both Hindus, for whom the cow was sacred, and Muslims, who felt defiled by contact with the pig (Judd 68–69). Behind the revolt was a "general suspicion" that the British intended a massive conversion of Indians to Christianity, a suspicion stimulated by "Christian missionary activity, by the prohibition of some traditional religious practices and by the introduction of Western education" (Wurgaft 4).[1]

Similarly, the September 11 attacks have been explained in terms of *jihad*, a holy war to remedy affronts to Islam, including the presence of American forces on the Arabian peninsula and America's support of Israel in its treatment of Palestinian Muslims. In both cases, then, the superpowers are portrayed as countries whose own spiritual and ethical beliefs are weakly held, and who, further, trample on the profound beliefs of others. Thus, the conflict is cast not in terms of land or resources or even political power, but as a battle of "good" against "evil," so that the superpowers are invited to perceive that it is not just their citizens or property that have been attacked but a cherished self image.

In both cases the atrocity of civilian death, as visited upon British citizens in India and American civilians – those who were at work in the World Trade Center, the Pentagon and flying on airliners – makes these events resemble the sort of intense personal attack that activates narcissistic anxieties, and that could make a response of "mature aggression" more difficult to achieve. In India, mutineers killed many European civilians, culminating with the notorious massacre at Cawnpore, where women and children were besieged for weeks under brutal conditions, offered safe passage on river boats, and then fired upon as they tried to board the boats. The survivors were re-imprisoned and finally, after horrific suffering, hacked to death, their bodies thrown down a well. On September 11, of course, thousands of civilians who had no direct connection to the attackers or their grievances other than that they were Americans flying in airplanes or working in buildings that were considered symbols of the country's economic and military power, were targeted and killed, many jumping to their deaths from the burning towers as those below watched in horror.

As if the fact of the deaths was not ghastly enough, messages sent by both sets of victims, who understood their impending doom, made the tragedy even more harrowing. As some of the besieged prisoners in India were able to record their experiences in notes written on walls of their prison, so workers who were on floors above the crash point in the World

Trade Center called family on cell phones to say that the ceilings of their offices were coming down, or that exits were blocked by fire. Those on board the doomed airliners made last calls to loved ones.

That the Indian "Mutiny" was perceived not as the action of an external foe, working toward its own purposes, but rather as a "deep wound upon the Victorian psyche" (Judd 66), is suggested by the fury of British retaliation which has been described as so "savage" and so obsessive as to be nearly "pornographic" (Druce 199). Villages were burned and thousands of Indians, including old men, women and children were killed so that the roads stank with rotting corpses. Many were executed, including boys "accused of romping around the city beating drums and flourishing rebel flags" (Ward 256). Before they were hanged, some Muslims were sewn into pigskins, "a vile and terrible fate for any follower of Islam." The mutineers who were "blown into fragments of flesh and bone from the mouths of cannon, or summarily hanged," Judd writes, "were among the lucky ones" (73).

At home, there was no will to restrain these "savage reprisals" (Kiernan 47), as the public was at the time and for years to come saturated to an astonishing degree with lurid accounts of the uprising, which became the subject of countless sermons, plays and poems, and about which more than eighty novels were written, six appearing in 1896 alone (Druce 197). Whipped to a fever pitch, some in the country demanded the "total subjugation of India" and even the "wholesale extermination" of Indians; Charles Dickens offered "genocide" as a solution to the problem (Brantlinger 208). With the uprising, the term "nigger" was, after a period of disuse, brought back into common parlance (Kiernan 48), and the *Times* described Nana Sahib, held to be the leader of the rebellion, as one of the "greatest enemies of the human race to the end of the world" (qtd. in Ward 512).

The excesses of the response to the uprising, which had never really threatened British rule (Judd 73), have frequently been remarked. V. G. Kiernan sees the event as causing the "sudden discovery by the British of their true position in India." After so many years of assuming an easy dominance of India, and viewing the natives as children who would eventually "learn to be thankful for the imperial presence," this event was a shock which "unbalance[ed]" the British (47). The uprising, thus, appeared not simply as a physical challenge to be put down, but as a terrifying assault upon the self-image of the British as benevolent rulers, an attack on the necessary assumption that British dominance was evident to all as a selfless mission to benefit others. Few, Patrick Brantlinger writes, saw the "Mutiny" as a "response to the greater violence of imperial domination" (218). Indeed, the view was expressed that the uprising was provoked by "the very virtues of the British rule . . . its cool justice, its steadfast enforcement of order" (204). The British, thus, in insisting that it was the very lofty selflessness of their mission that has been attacked, appear to demonstrate that the real target, as they understand it, has been their self-image and, as the hysteria of the response shows, this self-image was severely threatened. It is striking that the "basic fantasy" of the countless Mutiny-inspired fictions is that of "the imperialist dominators" becoming "victims and the dominated" (Brantlinger 222).

For most of Britain, it seems, the "Mutiny" did not provide a wake-up call to the rather unsurprising fact that people do not like to be ruled by others, however well these others might think of themselves. Rather, as the insistent use of the term "mutiny" implies, the uprising was seen as a betrayal. The Indians could not be recognized as pursuing their own independent aims, but rather as engaged in acts of treachery. As it could not be granted that there were rational reasons for rebelling against British rule, the explanation for the Indian actions had to be found in the inherent "evil" of their sexual appetites, with much of the literature of the "mutiny" obsessively suggesting that the rape of English women was a central aim of the rebels. Though there was no evidence that British women were raped – an act that would have violated the caste and religious proprieties of most Hindus and Muslims – this was the immediate and lasting assumption, and a great many of the novelizations of the event detailed the lascivious thoughts of Indians preparing to "'tear and mangle'" the white limbs of English women "in unspeakable tortures"(qtd. in Druce 199). So powerful was this belief, Ward writes, that the "merest suggestion . . . that English women were *not* raped" was considered by many at the time to be an outrage (675n).

One signal that such attacks are being read not only as a physical assault on national interests but also as the violation of a cherished self-image, is the rush to self-mythologize that follows. As the 19th century drew to a close, British empire, which had, at an earlier time, been viewed as a fairly straightforward for-profit venture, was increasingly portrayed as an expression of British racial and moral superiority. Popular performances and publications as well as works intended for children all extolled the glories of empire and the unique historical mission of the English (Castle 5). One example of this self-mythologizing, as noted earlier, was the revisionist view that was developed of medieval Britain. While in the 18th century, the medieval period was viewed as crude and barbaric, by the end of the 19th century the same period was viewed as a time of glory, adventure and heroism, and a prelude to the achievements of modern empire. This shift – the replacement of the mythology of the industrial revolution with the mythology of aristocratic and knightly virtues – may have done England actual economic harm, J. S. Bratton writes. The new mythology was a "self-defeating cultural maneuver" leading to England's failure to maintain its lead in industrialization (77). If the mythology of chivalry was not economically useful, it becomes even more likely that the impulse was psychological, the action of a people increasingly under pressure to support an unrealistic, grandiose self-image.

And what about the American response? Has America, in the face of attacks on both the physical and the theoretical America, healthily reasserted a rational sense of itself and its own goodness, or has it plunged into an orgy of panic-driven grandiosity? It is certain that following September 11 Americans of all sorts wrapped themselves in the flag in a way that would have been anathema during and after the Vietnam years. But how should this be read? Was this primarily a healthy expression of both mourning and love? Or should we view it as the frantic self-mythologizing of injured grandiosity?

It is also true that America responded to the September 11 attack with aggression, but has it been the "mature," rational aggression Kohut speaks of, or have Americans been driven by an irrational, retaliatory rage, to "undo the hurt by whatever means"?

Some of America's responses – such as the attacks on camps in Afghanistan where terrorists involved in the attacks were thought to have been trained – can be read rather easily as rational acts of self-defense. More questionable was the war on Iraq and what were later shown to have been false claims that Iraq had the capability to launch weapons of mass destruction, and that there was a connection between Iraq and September 11 terrorists. The decision to go to war in Iraq was made, perhaps, by a few, and theories abound as to what really propelled the Bush administration to attack. But whatever may have been working behind the scenes, it is clear that much of the country and the press backed the March 2003 "shock and awe" invasion of Iraq that, at least in its initial days, played on television like a sort of laser light show. At the time of the invasion, much of the public was ready to believe that terrorists were poised to use Iraqi weapons of mass destruction against America, and few were inclined to question what later proved to be remarkably flawed, sketchy, and perhaps manipulated intelligence. So much support for such a questionable and costly response seems to suggest the narcissist's urgent need to "undo the hurt by whatever means."

Finally, once cannot avoid being struck by the similarities between the atrocities reported after the Indian "Mutiny," and the revelations of humiliation and torture of Iraqi prisoners by American soldiers at the Abu Ghraib prison in Baghdad and perhaps in other locations. In both situations there was an emphasis on forcing prisoners to violate their own religious and moral beliefs. In India, Muslim men were wrapped in pigskin; at Abu Ghraib they were forced into humiliating sexual poses in what an independent panel called "acts of brutality and purposeless sadism" ("Findings"). Not only do such practices violate the principles of respect for fundamental human rights that the great democracies are supposed to stand for, but they also, at least in the American case, fail to produce useful results. Torture is not effective in eliciting good intelligence, experts have claimed, since under torture prisoners will frequently say whatever they think captors want to hear, not necessarily what is true. Nor do these brutal methods appear to have been effective in discouraging prospective terrorists; rather it is widely believed that images of American brutality are in effect recruiting tools for terrorists.

But if such horrific methods are not effective, why have they been so widely used? Reading through the lens of narcissistic theory, we must ask whether it is to some extent Muslim belief and world view itself that is attacked, as this belief and world view represents a "flaw" in America's "narcissistically perceived" reality. The assault upon Muslim manhood represented by sexual humiliations may be perceived on some level as a way of wiping away the doubts about American strength and goodness created by the 9/11 attacks into the heart of America.

All of us have grandiose tendencies that, if we are to live our lives sanely, must be tempered again and again by the realization that we are not always more brilliant, more powerful, more effortlessly dominant than others. As I write in the summer of 2006, the American self-mythologizing of three years ago has all but disappeared and along with it the approval for the war in Iraq that, as is widely acknowledge now, had little or nothing to do with the terrorists who attacked the country on September 11. Amid continued bloodshed and chaos in Iraq, the idea that America could impose its will on that country and the region through a brief display of "shock and awe" is long gone, and the prediction that America would be welcomed with "sweets" as noble liberators has become a cruel joke. Our grandiose ambitions appear to have been greatly tempered by events on the ground, perhaps bearing out George Orwell's claim that real war – as opposed to the fantasies of fear and dominance spun by rulers – keeps societies in touch with "physical reality" (197).

This will not be the first time America has seen its own favored self-image challenged. Again and again Americans have had to come up against the fact that we have denied to others the principles of freedom, equality and self-determination that we cherish for ourselves. Over time most Americans have conceded that the extermination of Native Americans was wrong, slavery was wrong, racial segregation was wrong, and we were wrong in Vietnam. In many ways, of course, we continue to profit by some of these actions; maybe we would take the same steps again if the opportunity arose. But, perhaps to a greater extent than was true of imperial Britain in the 19th century, we are in the habit of seeing our favored self-image challenged, and of messily but eventually surviving that challenge with our beliefs more or less intact. I allow myself to hope that our sense of our fundamental goodness, tempered by awareness of our failings, is real, not Kohut's "brittle" construct which will involve us in a terrifying and "unrestrained" pursuit of grandiose aims.

NOTES

Preface

1   The phrase is that of Wayland Young in *Eros Denied*, London, 1965.

1   *Loss, Rage and Revenge*

1   For an enraged discussion of the gap between the exalted portrait of England painted for school children in the colony of Antigua and the reality of England itself, see Jamaica Kincaid's essay, *On Seeing England for the First Time*.

2   Freud used the term "projection" to mean the imaginary expulsion of unwanted impulses so that these could be seen as located in others, rather than the self. Melanie Klein extended the concept to view that it is not just impulses but a part of the self that is now seen as located in another. The baby, Klein writes, views the mother's breast as sometimes good and sometimes bad. The breast is felt to be bad when it fails to provide for the child in the way he wishes, but also because "the baby projects its own aggression" onto the breast ("A Contribution" 40). D. W. Winnicott uses the term "projection" to describe the infant's view of the world "external to the self" as largely "based on the pattern of the personal inner reality."

3   Fairbairn uses "objects," a Freudian term for another person or part of a person, such as the breast or penis.

4   For an extensive analysis of Kohut and his work see Allen M. Siegel's *Heinz Kohut and the Psychology of the Self* (Routledge 1996).

5   For a brief discussion of the evolution of thought on narcissism, see "Landmark Contributions" in Andrew P. Morrison, ed., *Essential Papers on Narcissism*. In 1914, Freud, in an article, "On Narcissism: An Introduction," described "primary narcissism" as an "initial libidinal investment of psychic energy in the ego." We say, Freud wrote, "that a human being has originally two sexual objects – himself and the woman who nurses him – and in doing so we are postulating a primary narcissism in everyone" (Morrison 31).

Freud did not move beyond these initial thoughts, Morrison writes, and it was not until 1950 did further study on narcissism proceed.

Heinz Kohut's work is a departure from previous theories in that he questions the assumption made by previous authors that narcissism is fundamentally pathological. "Kohut argues that narcissism may lead, not only to object love, but also to more mature forms of narcissism, which he elaborates in terms of humor, creativity, empathy and wisdom" (Morrison, Andrew 15).

6 Kohut retains the terminology of classical psychoanalysis, Segal writes, in referring to the child's caretakers as objects. "As such they are experienced as part of the self and Kohut calls them selfobjects" (4).

7 Otto Kernberg is another leading theorist of narcissism. For comparative discussions of the views of Kernberg and Kohut see Mitchell and Black and also Andrew Morrison. Unlike Kohut, who eventually moved beyond Freud's drive theory, Kernberg sees "projection of oral rage" as central to the psychopathology of narcissists, whom he views as having "disturbances of their self regard and disturbed object relations and manifesting a high degree of self-reference in interaction with other people." Kernberg like Kohut emphasizes grandiosity but sees this as "inherently pathological" rather than, as does Kohut, a "normal developmental stage" (Morrison 168).

8 While there are no scientific studies of the psychological results of non-parental child care in the Victorian era that I am aware of, in our own time the largest study ever undertaken of non-parental child care has shown a correlation between hours spent in care and aggression and bullying behavior in children. In a study conducted by the U.S. National Institute of Child Health and Human Development, 1,300 children were tracked at ten sites across the country. Researchers found that a correlation between hours in care and aggressive attitudes held regardless of whether the children "came from rich or poor homes, were looked after by a relative, a nanny or at a center, and whether they were girls or boys." Children who spent more that thirty hours a week in child care "scored higher on items like 'gets in lots of fights,' 'cruelty,' 'explosive behavior,' as well as 'talking too much,' 'argues a lot,' and 'demands a lot of attention' and "more likely to be bullying kids,'" according to Jay Belsky of Birkbeck College, London, one of the lead investigators of the study (Vedantam).

9 Quote is from J. Richards, "'Passing the love of women'; manly love and Victorian society," in J. A. Mandan and J. Walvin (eds), *Manliness and Morality: Middle-Class Masculinity in Britain and America, 1800–1940*, Manchester 1987.

10 In Johnson's view, however, Kohut "overestim[ates] . . . the nuclear family as the context for psychic development," proceeding as if "the child had no independent experience of history, no relation to the world that is not filtered through parental images" (261). No matter how empathic the parenting, Johnson writes, parents cannot "offset the formative mirroring of the environment." A black child inserted into a hostile white environment would sustain "undeserved narcissistic injury," she claims, which could lead to the "kinds of precarious self-consolidation Larsen documents" (262).

2   *Thomas De Quincey*

1 De Quincey was notorious for making numerous revisions of his work. Here I use the earliest version of both "Confessions of an English Opium Eater" and "Suspiria de Profundis." "Confessions" first appeared in the *London*

Magazine in September and October 1821. "Suspiria" was first published in *Blackwood's Edinburgh Magazine* in 1845.

2   John Barrell, in his study, *The Infection of Thomas De Quincey*, uses Freudian theory to read that the seven-year-old Thomas experienced some sort of sexual guilt over the death of his sister, and seems to see unspecified sexual undertones in various situations including the boy's illicit viewing of his sister's dead body. Barrell, however, offers no specific evidence for this speculation, and I cannot see anything to support it. The desire for human warmth and affection, especially on the part of a child for whom these were in short supply, is a perfectly sufficient reason for seeking love and closeness. I agree with Barrell that De Quincey seems to feel guilt in connection with his sister's death, but I do not think there is cause to see it as sexual guilt. The sense that one has been too weak to save a loved one from disaster is a sufficient and common cause of guilt in survivors and is an attitude expressed in De Quincey's work.

3   In *Bush on the Couch: Inside the Mind of the President*, Justin Frank, a professor in the Department of Psychoanalysis at the George Washington University Medical Center, describes an event in the life of the young George W. Bush, which has interesting similarities to the emotional attitudes that surrounded De Quincey's loss of his sister, Elizabeth. In the spring of 1953, Bush's younger sister Robin was diagnosed with leukemia, which set into motion a series of extended East Coast trips by parents and child in the ultimately fruitless pursuit of treatment. "Critically, however," Frank writes, "the seven-year-old George W. was never informed of the reason for the absences; unaware that his sister was ill, he was simply told not to play with the girl, to whom he had grown quite close on her occasional visits home. Robin died in New York in October 1953; her parents spent the next day golfing in Rye, attending a small memorial service the following day before flying back to Texas. . . . There was no funeral."

This relatively disengaged style was typical of the future president's mother, Barbara, Frank writes, who reveals herself in her memoir, *Matriarch of a Dynasty*, as a "mother who leaves feelings behind, whose attitude ends discussion or curtails emotional engagement. On the morning after her husband lost his re-election effort to Bill Clinton, according to her son George's memoir, Barbara Bush uttered a single telling sentence: 'Well, now, that's behind us. It's time to move on.'"

4   For a fascinating discussion of opium, the role played by opium in cultural production, and its connection to British anxieties about intercourse with the East, see Barry Milligan's *Pleasures and Pains: Opium and the Orient in Nineteenth Century British Culture*. Milligan writes that De Quincey built upon the concept of opium as "the medium of a retributive Oriental infection-invasion" which was first expressed by Samuel Taylor Coleridge.

3   Robert Louis Stevenson

1   James Pope Hennessy suggests that the hostility to *The Amateur Emigrant* may be the result of middle-class Victorian prejudices. There is an "exceptional lack of snobbery" in the book, he writes. To Stevenson's father and to his London friends "his easy tolerance of people of a lower order must have

    seemed embarrassing and anarchic" and "in questionable taste" (148).

2   Fanny would often be described by Stevenson's British friends as a social climber, enamored of Stevenson's position in society and also of his father's wealth. If so, she must have also been something of a gambler to take a chance on the desperately ill, destitute, depressed and – at the time – disinherited, young man who came to her in California.

3   Stevenson's famous story has been read in a variety of ways over the years, as Katherine Linehan details in notes to her 2003 edition of *The Strange Case of Dr. Jekyll and Mr. Hyde.* In 1927, G. K. Chesterton read that the story demonstrated that "the load of man's moral struggle is bound upon him and cannot thus be escaped;" and that man cannot "cut himself off from his conscience." Wayne Koestenbaum in 1988 saw the story as based on homosexual energies, and as a "flight" from bourgeois narrative realism. Elaine Showalter in 1990 read that the "issue" in the story is "not Stevenson's 'real sexuality'" but rather "his sense of the fantasies beneath the surface of daylight decorum, the shadow of homosexuality that surrounds Clubland and the nearly hysterical terror of revealing forbidden emotions between men that constituted the dark side of patriarchy." In 1998 Patrick Brantlinger claimed that the story expresses "at least subliminally, anxiety about the masses and the consequences of mass literacy." In a reading that strikes me as having psychological similarities to my own, Katherine Linehan sees that Stevenson indicates that Jekyll "in ways he cannot see but bears responsibility for, remains every bit as much Hyde's author as he was in the beginning. . . . Stevenson leaves entrenched deep within the allegorical framework of the story the logic that refers Hyde's increasing demonism to the growth of fault made possible by Jekyll's abandonment of moral accountability."

4   Stevenson himself offered an analysis of the story in a letter written in response to a report of a 1887 New York City stage adaptation of *Jekyll and Hyde.* The story is not, he says, about sex: "The harm was in Jekyll because he was a Hypocrite. The Hypocrite let out the beast Hyde – who is no more sexual than another, but who is the essence of cruelty and malice, and selfishness and cowardice: and these are the diabolic in man – not this poor wish to have a woman that they make such a cry about" (qtd. in Linehan 86).

4 *Conan Doyle*

1   Conan Doyle would be close to his mother for the rest of her long life; fifteen hundred letters from Conan Doyle to his mother were at one time in the family archives. The picture of the relationship is complicated, however, by the numerous portraits of female seduction – especially the seduction of a young man by a much older woman – as dangerous and even fatal. In "The Ring of Thoth," a man dies as he embraces a beautiful, long-mummified woman: "So close was this embrace that it was only with the utmost difficulty that they were separated." The "extraordinary perversion of the theme surpasses Poe," Higham writes (59). In "The Parasite," a work Higham calls a "strikingly personal revelation of neurotic sexual obsession" (124), a young man is psychically imprisoned by a woman much older than himself and made to profess love, and even perhaps, though this is of course veiled, to make love to her. The man, who wishes to marry a sweet young girl, struggles fero-

ciously against this possession, going to the extreme of locking himself in his room and throwing the key out the window to keep himself from succumbing to the older woman's seductions. The love the woman has for him, the young man declares, is "monstrous, odious" ("Parasite" 82). When he is under her power he rejoices in his slavery; as her power wanes, however, his hate is as "bestial as the love. . . . It was the savage, murderous passion of the revolted serf" (91).

It is impossible to know what may have inspired such a story. It may be worth noting, however, that after the young Conan Doyle left home, his mother began a long association with a lodger she had taken in, Bryan Waller. Waller, who was a well-to-do medical student and six years older that Mary Doyle's son, is credited with keeping the family out of the poorhouse after Charles Doyle was hospitalized; eventually Mary Doyle and two of her daughters went to live with Waller on his country estate, where it was rumored that he was the father of her youngest daughter, who was also named Bryan.

2   For a discussion of themes of drugs and cannibalism as a source of foreign contamination in Conan Doyle's *The Sign of the Four* see Joseph McLoughlin's "The Romance of Invasion: Cocaine and Cannibals in 'The Sign of the Four'" in *Writing the Urban Jungle: Reading Empire in London From Doyle to Eliot* (Charlottesville, University of Virginia Press, 2000).

5   *Rudyard Kipling*

1   The poem is found as the heading to Chapter Four of *The Naulahka*, an adventure novel that Kipling wrote with his friend Wolcott Balestier in 1890. (Naulahka was also the name of he house the Kipling's built in Vermont; the $750 advance from the book was used to buy the plot of land upon which the house was built.)

Since the beginning of America's "war on terror" these lines have been cited by those skeptical of the ability of Western powers to ever truly dominate the East. Conservative writer Patrick Buchanan quotes the lines in an article posted on the website <www.antiwar.com> in April of 2004. Entitled "Kipling's Brutal Epitaph," the article asks, "Does [George Bush] comprehend the world he claims to be changing? Or is he inviting the brutal epitaph of Kipling?"

2   While there has been debate about the extent to which the story is autobiographical – it portrays the suffering of a five-year-old boy and his three-year-old sister who are returned from India and left for years with a brutal and unloving caregiver – the central facts of the story are indisputably those of Kipling's life. Further, Kipling's memoir, *Something of Myself*, appears to verify the account.

According to Kipling's biographer, Lord Birkenhead, the appearance of "Baa Baa, Black Sheep" in the Christmas 1888 edition of *The Week's News* was "a grievous blow to [Kipling's parents,] the Lockwood Kiplings when they read these savage outpourings in cold print, and, unwilling to recognize their own contribution to this suffering, they tried to make Trix [as Kipling's sister was called] say it was all exaggerated and untrue, but even to comfort them she could not pretend they had ever been happy" (qtd. in Pinney *Something* 135).

3   The poem, "A Song of White Men," is not often anthologized. I found it on a Newcastle University website which offers all of Kipling's poems. It is worth noting that the poem is also available on a website called "Ilovewhitefolks.com," along with "The White Man's Burden" and Kipling's "The Stranger," a poem which urges people to stay with their "own stock" even if "bitter bad they may be." Kipling is the only poet included on the site, which offers a variety of comment opposing integration and claiming the inferiority of non-whites.

6   Isak Dinesen

1   Blixen was ten years older than Mikhail Bakhtin, and *Seven Gothic Tales* was written in the early 1930s, ten years before Bakhtin submitted a doctoral thesis on Rabelais in which he focuses on carnival masking. Blixen's intention in her use of the mask, however, is in some ways similar: to defy power through masquerade. But Blixen's sense that disaster invariably befalls those who seek freedom through masking does not suggest the merriment that Bakhtin sees in the carnival masking. For Blixen, it is not authority that prevents the self from being revealed, but the fact that no coherent self can be located.

2   Many of those who had come to British East Africa were taking advantage of a British scheme to recoup British investment in a Mombasa-to-Kisume railroad by settling Kenya with Europeans. This line was built to clear a strategic passage to the headwaters of the Nile, thus protecting the Suez Canal and access to India, considered the jewel in the British imperial crown. To entice Europeans to Africa, prices were kept low so that immense amounts of land could be sold to investors. The area tended to attract a better-heeled class of immigrant, consequently, as a relatively high level of capitalization was needed to work such vast tracts of land.

3   Dinesen is not, of course, alone in imagining that the natives see the conquering Europeans as gods. But as Caroline Martin Shaw has shown in *Colonial Inscriptions: Race, Sex and Class in Kenya*, the Africans may have seen their conquerors in a different light than the Europeans imagined. "Getting a sense of what Africans thought of the early colonialists is not easy," Shaw writes, as "histories and ethnographies are obsessed with what happened rather than with the constitution of African subjectivity and the production of colonial discourse through African representation of the other." Shaw's own research, however, gathered by taking life histories of old Kikuyu men and women in Kenya, provides some evidence. "The first thing that almost all of them said to me in talking about the coming of the white people," Shaw writes, " was that the colonialists brought chiggers" (11).

Afterword

1   If the Indian uprising was triggered by a sense of religious affront over the greased cartridges, there were, of course, many other deep-rooted grievances.

As Judd writes, "the territorial annexations and reforming tendencies of the East India Company had affronted many sections of Indian society in the half century since the victorious conclusion of the Maratha Wars in 1818 had unquestionably established the British as the paramount power in the subcontinent. . . . Through the agency of the East India Company, the British had toppled Indian rulers, dispossessed landlords, and seemed to encourage attacks on the indigenous religious and cultural order. Changes such as improved rail and roadways seen as improvements by the British were seen by many Indians as high-handed and unwanted change. Proselytizing activity of Christian missionaries was read as an assault on religious practices. Further, relationships between British officers and Indian soldiers had worsened in the years prior to the uprising, with soldiers increasingly treated as racial inferiors" (69–70).

WORKS CITED

Abel, Elizabeth, ed. *Female Subjects in Black and White.* Berkeley: University of California Press, 1997.

Alcorn, Marshall. *Narcissism and the Literary Libido: Rhetoric, Text and Subjectivity.* New York: New York University Press, 1994.

Arlow, Jacob. "Object Concept and Object Choice." In Buckley, 127–46.

Balbus, Isaac D. "Masculinity and the (M)other: Toward a Synthesis of Feminist Mothering Theory and Psychoanalytic Theories of Narcissism." In Gardiner, 210–34.

Barfoot, C. C. ed. *Beyond Pug's Tour: National and Ethnic Stereotyping in Theory and Literary Practice.* Amsterdam: Rodopi, 1997.

Barrell, John. *The Infection of Thomas De Quincey: A Psychopathology of Imperialism.* New Haven: Yale University Press, 1991.

Berman, Jeffrey. *Narcissism and the Novel.* New York: New York University Press, 1990.

Bhabha, Homi. *The Location of Culture.* London: Routledge, 1994.

Birkenhead, Lord. *Rudyard Kipling.* London: Weidenfeld and Nicolson, 1978.

Bjornvig, Thorkild. "Who Am I? The Story of Isak Dinesen's Identity." In Pelensky, *Isak Dinesen: Critical Views,* 199–213.

Boehmer, Elleke. *Colonial and Postcolonial Literature: Migrant Metaphors.* Oxford: Oxford University Press, 1995.

Booth, Martin. *The Doctor and the Detective.* New York: Thomas Dunne, 1997.

Brantlinger, Patrick. *Rule of Darkness: British Literature and Imperialism, 1839–1914.* Ithaca: Cornell, 1988.

Bratton, J. S. "Of England, Home and Duty: The Image of England in Victorian and Edwardian Juvenile Fiction." In MacKenzie, 73–93.

Bristow, Joseph. *Empire Boys: Adventures in a Man's World.* London: HarperCollins Academic, 1991.

Bronte, Charlotte. *Jane Eyre.* 1847. London: Penguin, 1985.

Buckley, Peter M.D., ed. *Essential Papers in Object Relations.* New York: New York University Press, 1986.

Calder, Jenni. "The Eyeball of the Dawn." In Jones, 7–19.

——. *Robert Louis Stevenson: A Life Study.* New York: Oxford University Press, 1980.

Carrington, Charles. *The Life of Rudyard Kipling*. Garden City, New York: Doubleday, 1955.

Castle, Kathryn. *Britannia's Children: Reading Colonialism Through Children's Books and Magazines*. Manchester: Manchester University Press, 1996.

Césaire, Aimé. *Discourse on Colonialism*. 1955. New York: Monthly Review Press, 1972.

Chandos, John. *Boys Together: English Public Schools 1890–1864*. New Haven: Yale, 1984.

Chesterton, G.K. *Robert Louis Stevenson*. New York: Dodd Mead, 1928.

Chodorow, Nancy J. *The Reproduction of Mothering*. Berkeley: University of California Press, 1978.

De Quincey, Thomas. "China." In *The Works of Thomas De Quincey*, Vol. 12. Boston: Houghton Mifflin, 1877. 166–267.

——. "The Chinese Question in 1857." In *The Collected Writings of Thomas de Quincey*, Vol. 14. Edinburgh: Adam and Charles Black, 1890, 345–67.

——. "Confessions of an English Opium-Eater." In Lindop *Confessions*, 1–85.

——. "The Opium Question with China in 1840." In *The Collected Writings of Thomas De Quincey*. Vol. 14. Edinburgh: Adam and Charles Black, 1890, 162–216.

——. "Suspiria de Profundis." In Lindop *Confessions*, 87–233.

Dervin, Daniel. "Lacanian Mirrors and Literary Reflection." *Journal of the Philadelphia Association for Psychoanalysis* 7 (1996): 129–42.

Dickens, Charles. *David Copperfield*. 1849, 1850. New York: Signet, 1980.

Dinesen, Isak. *Out of Africa* and *Shadows on the Grass*. 1937,1960. New York: Vintage Books, 1985.

——. *Seven Gothic Tales*. 1934. New York: Vintage International, 1991.

Doyle, Arthur Conan. *Sherlock Holmes: The Complete Novels and Stories*. 2 Vols. New York: Bantam, 1986.

——. "The Parasite." *Forgotten Fantasy: Classics of Science Fiction and Fantasy*. 1:1 (1970): 65–107.

Druce, Robert. "National and Racial Stereotypes in the British Raj." In Barfoot, 183–212.

Ellis, Sarah Strickney. *The Women of England: Their Social Duties and Domestic Habits*. London: Fisher and Son, 1839.

Erikson, Erik. *Childhood and Society*. 1950. New York: W.W. Norton, 1993.

——. *Young Man Luther: A Study in Psychoanalysis and History*. 1958, 1962. New York: W. W. Norton, 1993.

Fairbairn, W. R. D. *Psychoanalytic Studies of the Personality*. 1952. London: Routledge, 1992.

Fanon, Frantz. *Black Skin, White Masks*. 1952. New York: Grove, 1967.

Fay, Peter Ward. *The Opium War 1840–1842*. New York: Norton, 1975.

"Findings on Abu Ghraib Prison: Sadism, 'Deviant Behavior' and Failure of Leadership." *The New York Times*, 25 August 2004: A 10.

Frank, Justin A. *Bush on the Couch: Inside the Mind of the President*. New York: Regan Books, 2004.

Fraser, Robert. *Victorian Quest Romance: Stevenson, Haggard, Kipling, and Conan Doyle*. Plymouth, UK: Northcote House, 1988.

Freud, Sigmund. *The Standard Edition of the Complete Psychoanalytic Works of Sigmund Freud*, Vol. 1. London: The Hogarth Press, 1966.

Gathorne-Hardy, Jonathan. *The Rise and Fall of the English Nanny*. London: Hodder and Stoughton, 1972.

Girouard, Mark. *The Return to Camelot: Chivalry and the English Gentleman*. New Haven: Yale University Press, 1981.

Gardiner, Judith Kegan, ed. *Masculinity Studies & Feminist Theory*. New York: Columbia University Press, 2002.

Guntrip, Harry. *Personality Structure and Human Interaction*. New York: International Universities Press, 1961.

Haining, Peter. *The Penny Dreadful*. London: Victor Gollancz, 1975.

Harris, Jose. *Private Lives, Public Spirit: Britain 1870–1914*. London: Penguin, 1994.

Hennessy, James Pope. *Robert Louis Stevenson*. New York: Simon and Schuster, 1974.

Herman, Judith. *Basic Books*. New York: Perseus, 1997.

Higham, Charles. *The Adventures of Conan Doyle*. New York: W.W. Norton, 1976.

Hobsbawm, Eric. *The Age of Empire: 1875–1914*. New York: Vintage, 1989.

Hodgson, John. A., ed. *Sherlock Holmes: The Major Stories with Contemporary Critical Essays*. Boston: Bedford, 1994.

Holland, Norman. "The Trouble(s) With Lacan." 1998. <www.clas. ufl.edu/users /nnh/lacan.htm>.

Hughes, Judith M. *Reshaping the Psychoanalytic Domain: The Work of Melanie Klein, W. R. D. Fairbairn & D.W. Winnicott*. Berkeley: University of California Press, 1989.

Hunt, David. *Parents and Children in History: The Psychology of Family Life in Early Modern France*. New York: Basic Books, 1970.

Hyam, Ronald. *Empire and Sexuality*. Manchester: Manchester University Press, 1990.

Ibsen, Henrik. *Four Major Plays*. Vol. 1. New York: Signet, 1965.

James, Henry. "The Art of Fiction." Published in *Longman's Magazine* (September 1884). <www.mantex.co.uk/ou/aa810/james-05.htm>, June 12, 2002.

JanMohamed, Abdul R. "*Out of Africa*: The Generation of Mythic Consciousness." In Pelensky, *Isak Dinesen: Critical Views*, 138–56.

Jeffries, Dexter. Letter to the author. 1 March 2001.

Johnson, Barbara. "The Quicksands of the Self: Nella Larsen and Heinz Kohut." In Abel 252–65.

Jones, William B. Jr., ed. *Robert Louis Stevenson Reconsidered: New Critical Perspectives*. Jefferson, N.C.: McFarland, 2003.

Jolly, Roslyn, ed. *Robert Louis Stevenson: South Sea Tales*. Oxford: Oxford University Press, 1996.

Judd, Denis. *Empire: The British Imperial Experience from 1765 to the Present*. New York: Basic Books, 1996.

Kane, Penny. *Victorian Families in Fact and Fiction*. New York: Macmillan, 1995.

Kegan, Judith. "Self Psychology as Feminist Theory." *Signs* 12.4: 761–80.

Kernberg, Otto. "Further Contributions to the Treatment of Narcissistic Personalities." *International Journal of Psycho-Analysis* 55 (1974): 215–40.

Kiernan, V. G. *The Lords of Human Kind: Black Man, Yellow Man, and White Man in an Age of Empire.* London: Weidenfield and Nicolson, 1969.

Kincaid, Jamaica. "On Seeing England for the First Time." In Best American Essays 1992. Susan Sontag, ed. Boston: Houghton Mifflin, 1992, 209–20.

———. "Ovando." *Conjunctions* 14: 75–83.

Kipling, Rudyard. *American Notes.* New York: The Lowell Company, 1889.

———. "Baa Baa, Blacksheep." In Raine, 87–110.

———. *Gunga Din and Other Favorite Poems.* New York: Dover, 1990.

———. *The Jungle Book.* 1894. London: Penguin, 1987.

———. *Kim.* 1901. New York: Bantam, 1983.

———. *The Light That Failed.* 1891. New York: Penguin, 1988.

———. *Plain Tales from the Hills.* 1890. London: Penguin, 1990.

———. "A Sahib's War." In Raine, 206–20.

———. *Soldiers Three* and *In Black and White.* London: Penguin, 1993.

———. *Something of Myself.* In Pinney, *Something.* 3–102.

———-"Song of White Men." <http://whitewolf.newcastle.edu. au/words/K/ KiplingRudyard/verse/p1/whitemen.html>.

Klein, Melanie. "A Contribution to the Psychogenesis of Manic-Depressive States." In Buckley, 40–70.

———. *Love, Guilt and Reparation and Other Works 1921–1945.* New York: Free Press, 1975.

Knight, Stephen. "The Case of the Great Detective." In Hodgson, 368–80.

Kohut, Heinz and Ernest S. Wolf. "The Disorders of the Self and Their Treatment: An Outline." In Andrew Morrison, 175–96.

Kohut, Heinz. "Forms and Transformations of Narcissism." In Andrew Morrison, 61–88.

———. "Thoughts on Narcissism and Narcissistic Rage." In Ornstein, 615–58.

Koestenbaum, Wayne. "The Shadow on the Bed: Dr. Jekyll, Mr. Hyde and the Labouchere Amendment." *Critical Matrix* (Spring 1988): 31–55.

Lacan, Jaques. *Ecrits: A Selection.* New York: W.W. Norton, 1977.

Lane, Christopher, ed. *The Psychoanalysis of Race.* New York: Columbia, 1998.

Langbaum, Robert. "Autobiography and Myth in African Memoirs." In Pelensky, *Isak Dinesen: Critical Views,* 38–50.

Lasson, Frans. *Isak Dinesen: Letters From Africa 1914–1931.* Chicago: University of Chicago Press, 1978.

Layton, Lynn and Barbara Ann Schapiro, eds. *Narcissism and the Text: Studies in Literature and the Psychology of Self.* New York: New York University Press, 1986.

Lindop, Grevel. *Confessions of an English Opium Eater and Other Writings.* Oxford: Oxford University Press, 1996.

———. *The Opium-Eater: A Life of Thomas De Quincey.* New York: Taplinger, 1981.

Linehan, Katherine, ed. *Strange Case of Dr. Jekyll and Mr. Hyde.* New York: W.W. Norton, 2003.

Lochhead, Marion. *Their First Ten Years: Victorian Childhood.* London: John Murray, 1956.

McClintock, Anne. *Imperial Leather: Race, Gender and Sexuality in the Colonial Contest.* New York: Routledge, 1995.

Mackenzie, John M., ed. *Imperialism and Popular Culture.* Manchester: Manchester University Press, 1986.

McLoughlin, Joseph. *Writing the Urban Jungle: Reading Empire in London from Doyle to Eliot.* Charlottesville: University of Virginia Press, 2000.

McGivering, John. "Baa Baa, Black Sheep." <www.kipling.org.uk/rg_ baabaa1_p.htm>.

Mannoni, Octave. *Prospero and Caliban: The Psychology of Colonization.* 1950. New York: Frederick A. Praeger, 1956.

Marshall, Dr. Peter. *Sex, Nursery Rhymes, and Other Evils.* Vancouver: Whitecap, 1995.

Memmi, Albert. *The Colonizer and the Colonized.* 1957. Boston: Beacon Press, 1967.

Menikoff, Barry, ed. *Robert Louis Stevenson: Tales from the Prince of Storytellers.* Evanston: Northwestern University Press, 1993.

Miller, Alice. "Depression and Grandiosity as Related Forms of Narcissistic Disturbance." In Andrew Morrison, 323–47.

——. *The Drama of the Gifted Child.* 1979. New York: Basic Books, 1981.

Miller, John. "Greetings, America. My Name is Osama bin Laden." *Esquire,* February 1999. <www.esquire.com/feat . . . articles/2001/010913_mfe_ binladen_6. html>.

Milligan, Barry. *Pleasures and Pains: Opium and the Orient in Nineteenth Century British Culture.* Charlottesville: University of Virginia Press, 1995.

Mintz, Steven. *A Prison of Expectations: The Family in Victorian Culture.* New York: New York University Press, 1983.

Mitchell, Stephan A. and Margaret J. Black. *Freud and Beyond: A History of Modern Psychoanalytic Thought.* New York: Basic Books, 1995.

Morrison, Andrew. *Essential Papers on Narcissism.* New York: New York University Press, 1986.

Morrison, Toni. *Playing in the Dark: Whiteness and the Literary Imagination.* New York: Random House, 1992.

Nelson, Claudia. "Growing Up: Childhood." In Tucker, 69–81.

Ngugi wa Thiong'o. *Barrel of a Pen: Resistance to Repression in Neo-Colonial Kenya.* Trenton, N.J. : African World Press, 1983.

——. *Weep Not, Child.* 1964. London: Heinemann, 1987.

Ornstein, Paul. H., ed. *The Search for the Self: Selected Writings of Heinz Kohut: 1950–1978.* Vol. 2. New York: International Universities Press, 1978.

Orwell, George. *1984.* 1949. New York: Signet, 1977.

Pelensky, Olga Anastasia, ed. *Isak Dinesen: Critical Views.* Athens, Ohio: Ohio University Press, 1993.

——. *Isak Dinesen: The Life and Imagination of a Seducer.* Athens, Ohio: Ohio University Press, 1991.

Pinney, Thomas, ed. *The Letters of Rudyard Kipling: Vol. 1: 1872–1889.* Iowa: University of Iowa Press, 1990.

——, ed. *Something of Myself and other Autobiographical Writings.* New York: Cambridge University Press, 1990.

Porter, Bernard. *Critics of Empire: British Radical Attitudes to Colonialism in Africa 1895–1914*. London: Macmillan, 1968.

——.*The Lion's Share: A Short History of British Imperialism* 1850–1895. New York: Longman, 1996.

Raine, Craig, ed. *A Choice of Kipling's Prose*. London: Faber and Faber, 1987.

Rabin, Jonathan. Introduction. *The Amateur Immigrant*. London: The Hogarth Press, 1984.

Ricketts, Harry. *Rudyard Kipling: A Life*. New York: Carroll & Graf, 1999.

Rising, Catherine. *Darkness at Heart: Fathers and Sons in Conrad*. New York: Greenwood, 1990.

Rutherford, Jonathan. *Reflections on Masculinity and Empire*. London: Lawrence & Wishart, 1997.

Shaw, Carolyn Martin. *Colonial Inscriptions: Race, Sex and Class in Kenya*. Minneapolis: University of Minnesota Press, 1995.

Showalter, Elaine. *Sexual Anarchy: Gender and Culture at the Fin de Siècle*. New York: Viking, 1990.

Siegel, Allen M. *Heinz Kohut and the Psychology of the Self*. London: Routledge, 1996.

Stashower, Daniel. *Teller of Tales: The Life of Arthur Conan Doyle*. New York: Henry Holt, 1999.

Stern, Daniel. *The Interpersonal World of the Infant: A View from Psychoanalysis and Developmental Psychology*. New York: Basic Books, 1985

Stevenson, Robert Louis. *A Child's Garden of Verses*. <www.kellscraft. com/childsvers.html>.

——. *The Complete Short Stories of Robert Louis Stevenson*. Charles Neider, ed. New York: Doubleday, 1969.

——. *Dr. Jekyll and Mr. Hyde*. 1886. New York: Penguin, 1978.

——. *Ebb Tide*. New York: Grosset and Dunlap, 1893.

——. *In the South Seas*. 1896. London: Penguin, 1998.

——. *Kidnapped*. 1886. New York: Bantam, 1982.

——. *Memoirs of Himself*. Printed from the original by Harry Elkin Widener. Private Distribution. Philadelphia, 1912. New York Public Library Rare Books Collection.

——. *Memories and Portraits*. London: Nelson, 1905.

——. *New Arabian Nights*. New York: Grolier Club, 1923.

——. *Treasure Island*. 1883. New York: Dover, 1985.

Suleri, Sara. *The Rhetoric of English India*. Chicago: University of Chicago Press, 1992.

Sullivan, Zohreh. *Narratives of Empire: The Fictions of Rudyard Kipling*. New York: Cambridge University Press, 1993.

Thurman, Judith. *Isak Dinesen: The Life of a Storyteller*. New York: Picador, 1995.

Tucker, Herbert F., ed. *A Companion to Victorian Literature and Culture*. Oxford: Blackwell, 1999.

Vedantam, Shankar. "Child aggressiveness study cites day care." *The Washington Post*. April 19, 2001. <www.childcarecanada.org/ccin/2001/ccin04_19_01.html>.

Ward, Andrew. *Our Bones Are Scattered: The Cawnpore Massacres and the Indian Mutiny of 1857*. New York: Henry Holt, 1996.

West, Edward Sackville. *Thomas De Quincey: His Life and Works*. New Haven: Yale University Press, 1936.

Wilson, Angus. *The Strange Ride of Rudyard Kipling*. New York: Viking, 1997.

Wilson, Edmund. *The Wound and the Bow*. 1929. Athens, OH: Ohio University Press, 1997.

Winnicott, D.W. *The Family and Individual Development*. 1965. London: Routledge, 1995.

———. "The Theory of Parent–Infant Relationship." *International Journal of Psychoanalysis*. 41 (1960): 585–95.

Wolff, Richard D. *Economics of Colonialism*. New Haven: Yale University Press, 1974.

Wurgaft, Lewis. *The Imperial Imagination: Magic and Myth in Kipling's India*. Middletown, CT: Wesleyan, 1983.

Young, Wayland. *Eros Denied: Sex in Western Society*. New York: Grove Press, 1964.

Young-Bruehl, Elisabeth. *The Anatomy of Prejudices*. Cambridge, MA: Harvard University Press, 1996.

INDEX

Index

Judy (fictional character), 92
Jungle Books (Kipling), 92

Kane, Penny, 9
Kasparson (fictional character), 102, 104–105
Kegan, Judith, 25
Kenya, viii, 22, 99, 100, 108, 110, 131n2 (chap. 6), 131n3 (chap. 6)
Kernberg, Otto, 25, 127n7 (chap. 1)
Khan, Azimulla, 116, 118
Kidnapped (Stevenson), 47
Kiernan, V.G., 121
Kikuyu, 109, 110, 131n3 (chap. 6)
Kim (fictional character), 77–78, 80, 93, 97–98
Kim (Kipling), 77–78, 80, 93, 97–98
Kincaid, Jamaica, 126n1 (chap. 1)
Kingston, William, 18
Kipling, Rudyard: and America, 93, 94, 91, 98; and boarding school, 86; and Boer War, 95–98; childhood of, 82, 83–87, 92–95, 97; and depression, 81, 94; and Dickens, 82; and dreams, 98; on empire, 81–82, 90–91, 94–95; and grandiosity, ix, 81, 97; career in India, 81; and loss, 81; and narcissism, 91–92, 97, 98; and propaganda, 95; and racism, 80–82, 95; and rage, 81, 95; and revenge, 80–81; and women, 89. *See also individual works and specific fictional characters*
Kipling, Trix, 82, 84, 92, 130n2 (chap. 5)
Kitosch, 112–113
Klein, Melanie, 2–3, 126n2 (chap. 1)
Knight, Stephen, 67, 69
knights and knightly virtues, 51, 65–66, 68, 76–77, 79, 122–23
Koestenbaum, Wayne, 129n3 (chap. 3)
Kohut, Heinz: on adult ego, 101; on aggression, ix-x, 95–97, 115–116, 123; analysis of his work, 126n4 (chap. 1); on authority, narcissistic, viii, 7; on caregivers, 14, 127n6 (chap. 1); on child development, 5–6; compared to other scholars, 127n7 (chap. 1), 127n10 (chap. 1); on disturbance, narcissistic, 15; on injury, narcissistic, ix-x; and Lacan, 25; narcissist characterized by, 36, 95, 100–101, 127n5 (chap 1);); on creation of narcissists, 100–110; an object relations theorist, 25; on parental role, 5, 6, 8, 10; on psycho-analysis, 24; on rage, ix-x, 96, 97, 116; on revenge, narcissistic, 40
Koran, 109
Kurtz (fictional character), 61

Lacan, Jacques, 25–27, 82
Lane, Christopher, 22
Langbaum, Robert, 108
language (concept), vii, 26
Leask, Nigel, 40
"Legend of Hitler's Childhood, The" (Erikson), 17
Life magazine, 113
Light that Failed, The (Kipling), 82, 89, 91
Lin (Comissioner of Canton), 42
Lindop, Grevel, 30
Linehan, Katherine, 129n3 (chap. 3)
"Lispeth" (Kipling), 88
Lochhead, Marion, 10
"Lodging for the Night, A" (Stevenson), 51, 61
London Magazine, 127–28n1 (chap. 2)
London Times, 64
loss: and Blixen, 60, 100, 101, 102, 105, 106; and children, 3; and depression, 7; and Doyle, 68, 71, 76, 78; and imperialism, 17, 19, 23; and Kipling, 81, 82, 92, 94, 97; and maternal, 15; and narcissism, 1, 7, 8; and personal past, viii; and Stevenson, 53; and Wilde, 64
Lost World, The (Doyle), 78
Lovborg, Eilert (fictional character), 112
love: not admiration, 7; and Blixen, 60, 99, 100, 101, 102, 103, 104, 105, 106, 107, 108, 109, 110; and children, 7; and De Quincey, 30, 31, 34, 39, 40, 43, 128n2 (chap. 2); and Doyle, 70, 71, 129–30n1 (chap. 3); and Freud, 3; and Kipling, 84, 86, 87, 89, 91, 95–96, 97; manly, 127n9 (chap. 1); of mother, 7, 30; and nanny, 10; and object, 127n5 (chap. 1); and "Parasite, The" (Doyle), 129–30n1 (chap. 3); and parents, 9; and self, 5; and September 11, 2001, 123; and Stevenson, 51, 57, 61

MacKenzie, John M., 18–19, 44, 45
Malay (fictional character), 35–36
Mannoni, Octavo, 19–22
Maratha Wars, 131–32n1 (Afterword)
Marner, Silas (fictional character), 9
Marshall, Peter, 14
masculinity, 46, 59 fig.
masks, viii, 8, 22, 99, 100, 104, 108, 110, 131n1 (chap. 6)
Matriarch of a Dynasty (Bush), 128n3 (chap. 2)
McClintock, Anne, 19, 27
McClure, Sam, 57
McLoughlin, Joseph, 130n2 (chap. 4)
Memmi, Albert, 20, 61